GARDENS
of *Dorset*

ROGER LANE

GARDENS

of Dorset

ROGER LANE

F

FRANCES LINCOLN LIMITED
PUBLISHERS

Frances Lincoln Limited
4 Torriano Mews
Torriano Avenue
London NW5 2RZ
www.franceslincoln.com

Gardens of Dorset
Copyright © Frances Lincoln Limited 2010
Text and photographs copyright © Roger Lane 2010
First Frances Lincoln edition 2010

A catalogue record for this book is available from the British Library.

978-0-7112-3090-3

Printed and bound in China
2 7 6 8 9 8 5 3 1

CONTENTS

PREVIOUS PAGES View through the trees near Raleigh's Seat at Sherborne Castle.
LEFT A relaxing English garden scene at The Ferns.

LOCATION MAP

The majority of the gardens in this book open under the National Gardens Scheme. For details, see *The Yellow Book: NGS Gardens Open for Charity*, published annually by the National Gardens Scheme (www.ngs.org.uk).

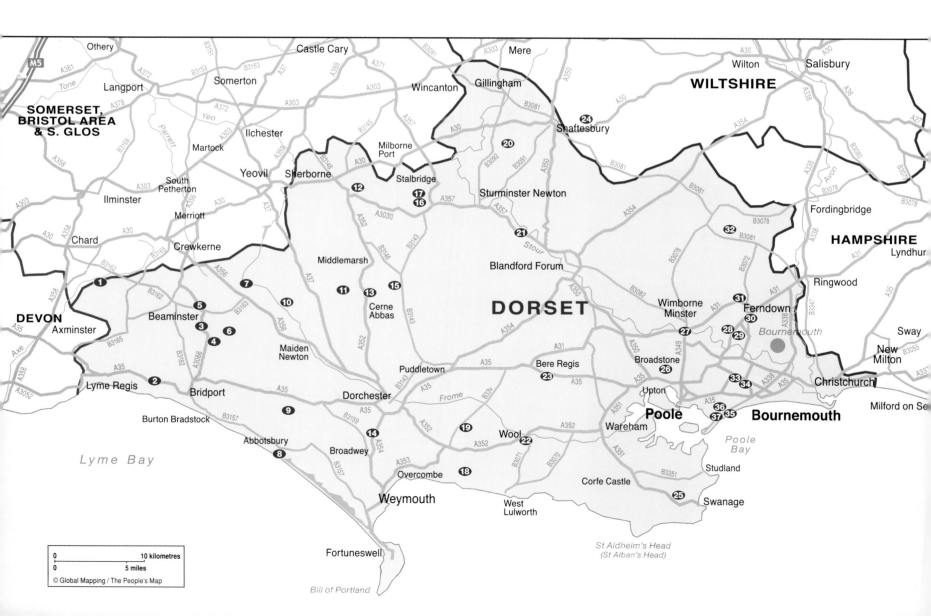

© Global Mapping / The People's Map

Dahlia 'El Paso'.

INTRODUCTION

Without doubt my home county of Dorset is extremely rich in the diversity of its landscape. From its Jurassic coastline of World Heritage status featuring such unique places as Chesil Beach and Portland Bill, to the rolling chalk hills of its hinterland and the rich pastures of Blackmore and Marshwood Vales, there are views that have delighted travellers and inspired artists for centuries. Wordsworth and Turner have succumbed to Dorset's landscape, and its great heaths have also been immortalized in the novels of Thomas Hardy.

Within this varied landscape are other pockets of history, colour and inspiration. These include the gardens of Dorset, large and small. Some have historic origins, inevitably surrounding a manor or estate, while others have been inspired by the existence of natural elements – providing some surprises. Who, for example, would expect to find a frost-free subtropical garden within sight and sound of the English Channel, yet only a few minutes' drive away from a true English country garden full of roses and peonies?

Dorset receives its fair share of sunshine, not a particularly heavy rainfall but of course the inevitable sea mists. The coastline releases fresh sea breezes, even in the hottest of summers, and these provide a subtlety of temperature without humidity. This gentle climate can be regarded by gardeners as almost perfect. However, there can be rare moments of extremes and the county has at times suffered the ravages of severe gales.

Within the county's 900 square miles/2,330 square kilometres, Dorset soils provide the lifeblood for its gardens. Chalk downland runs from Shaftesbury south-west towards the coast at Lyme Regis. Clay can be found in the vales and river valleys, where it varies constantly, from the Kimmeridge clay in the south to the Oxford clays in the north and east. Sandy soils are another vital element, underpinning the heathland that adds yet another dimension to the wonderfully varied landscape.

In this book I have sought to provide a portfolio of Dorset gardens, most of which are included in the National Garden Scheme (NGS). This scheme allows talented gardeners to exhibit their enthusiasm and creative abilities by opening their gardens to the public at varied times throughout the year in aid of NGS-designated charities. There are currently more than ninety gardens in Dorset open to the public under the scheme. Regrettably, it has not been possible to feature all of them in this book. Indeed, a number of Dorset's gardens have not been included at the owner's request; some wished to provide gardening pleasure to visitors in their own personal way, while others were undergoing periods of restoration and replanting. However, those gardens who accepted the invitation to be included provide a rich tapestry of garden effects. They range in style from the historical and formal through those with Mediterranean and Far Eastern influences to the more rural and traditional.

Travelling more than 2,000 miles/3,220 kilometres through the county with my former colleague and contributing author Phil Wills to photograph the gardens of Dorset sometimes became a race against weather and light, but the experience was an entirely pleasurable one. Finding oneself in a garden full of inner landscapes is a photographer's dream. For where better to explore the challenge of capturing the elusive elements of light and composition than in a garden, where the design itself is an expression of art? At the end of this journey, I trust that in some small way the images and stories I have been privileged to record will allow you to follow in our footsteps and enjoy the magnificence of these gardens. I wish you all an enjoyable tour.

Roger Lane, November 2009

The Italian garden at Compton Acres in its summer splendour.

FORDE ABBEY, CHARD

Eight-hundred-year-old Forde Abbey, a converted Cistercian monastery on the boundary between Dorset and Somerset, is surrounded by some 30 acres/12 hectares of gardens. Developed through years of private ownership, these live harmoniously and informally with their historical connections and provide seasonal colour and interest in a most pleasing and natural way.

Built in 1148, the abbey flourished as a seat of learning. The third abbot, Abbot Baldwin, became Archbishop of Canterbury before losing his life in the Crusades. His successor, John Devonius, became confessor to King John and was reputedly the most learned man in the country. By then, Forde had become a wealthy foundation; however, on the dissolution of the larger monasteries the then abbot, Thomas Chard, decided that discretion was the better part of valour and in 1539 handed the abbey to the Crown.

Following a succession of absentee landlords, in 1649 Edmund Prideaux, MP for Lyme Regis and attorney to Oliver Cromwell, purchased the abbey and turned it into a private home. In 1659 he was succeeded by his son, also named Edmund, who made the mistake of entertaining the Duke of Monmouth at Forde. When Monmouth's rebels were defeated at the Battle of Sedgemoor, Prideaux was arrested for high treason and imprisoned in the Tower of London. Placating the notorious Judge Jeffries with the sum of £15,000, he escaped the gallows and returned to Forde, where he lived until his death in 1702.

His daughter Margaret inherited the estate, and it was she, with her husband, Francis Gwyn, who began creating the garden that we see today. It is believed that they were advised by Monsieur Beaumont, a pupil of André Le Nôtre,

A view of the abbey from the Park Garden.

The fountain in the Mermaid Pond is the tallest powered fountain in England.

who was famously responsible for the design of the Jardin des Tuileries in Paris and the park at Versailles. The Gwyns' successors continued to live in the house, but died out in 1846, when it was sold to a Mr Miles, who regrettably neglected it. A further sale in 1864 brought the abbey into the ownership of the Evans family, who embarked on a programme of restoration, designing the gardens in the Victorian style of the day. Through bequests and marriage, the estate passed to the Roper family. Their descendants, Mark Roper and his sister Charlotte, assisted by members of staff, present these magnificent gardens to the public today.

You enter through the Kitchen Garden, where the monks would have grown their vegetables; today the area produces fruit, vegetables and cut flowers for the house and tearoom. Next you go into the Abbey Yard, where roses are interplanted with a variety of flowers providing seasonal interest. A left turn takes you through an archway to the east side of the house, where on either side mature wisterias – *W. sinensis* and *W. floribunda* 'Macrobotrys' – adorn the walls. Along the front of the house, flowerbeds, which form the cloister garth, replace those that in monastic times would have been planted

Meconopsis napaulensis and *Primula alpicola* are among the plants in the Bog Garden.

with herbs for medicinal and culinary purposes.

From here you come to the Long Pond and, running parallel to it, the Herbaceous Border. Punctuated by yews planted by the Evans family, the border is at its best from July onwards, with a changing display of plants. Walking alongside the Long Pond you see three cascades falling in line from the Great Pond (at the top of the garden), the Canal Pond and the Mermaid Pond. While the Great Pond is the only structure to remain from monastic times, the cascades and lower ponds were created by Francis Gwyn. The Mermaid Pond has the tallest powered fountain in the country, which exhibits a plume of water some 160 feet/49 metres high daily at fifteen-minute intervals between 12.00 and 3.00 p.m. (weather permitting). Formally opened in 2005 by the radio presenter Anne Swithinbank, it celebrates 100 years of the Roper family

at Forde Abbey. At the western end of the Long Pond a more recent addition to the garden stands in all its glory: a *tempietto*, constructed in Ham stone by local craftsmen, with an ornate wrought-iron dome that is reflected in the pond.

Heading south towards the Great Pond, you find the Bog Garden, which Mark Roper has rejuvenated and replanted. It now provides a brightly coloured display of Candelabra primulas during May and June. The Great Pond is close by, covering an area of around 3 acres/1.25 hectares. The beech house on its northern shore was created in the 1930s as a bird-watching hide, made entirely from pleached beech.

Returning towards the park and the top lawns, you come to the ha-ha, which separates the park from the lawns. The Gwyns created this in the eighteenth century to keep out animals while maintaining the view of the park from the house. In the eastern part of the garden is an avenue of red-twigged limes (*Tilia platyphyllos* 'Rubra'), planted by Geoffrey Roper in 1936 to celebrate the birth of his first-born son, Mark,

Early spring crocuses in the park.

and a magnificent arboretum, another legacy from Geoffrey Roper, with a fine collection of trees and shrubs, including varieties of hamamelis, camellia, rhododendron, magnolia and embothrium, as well as a rare *Picea farreri*, which came to Forde Abbey from Burma via Exbury Gardens in Hampshire. During his time at Forde, Geoffrey Roper planted more than 350,000 trees on the estate.

The Rock Garden contains a mixture of rock and alpine plants, a *Cornus controversa* underplanted with *Lilium pyrenaicum* and a display of cyclamen earlier in the year. Next to it is the Park Garden, an area of mainly herbaceous plants with spring shrubs. Hellebores grow under the west wall during early spring and two central beds contain wallflowers and tulips. Perhaps most of all, Forde Abbey is renowned for its carpet of *Crocus vernus* and *C. tommasinianus*, which covers more than 10 acres/4 hectares of the garden in early spring – a sight that welcomes both visitors and a new season to the garden.

The Rock Garden, created in 1923 with rocks unearthed from the estate, is planted with a mixture of alpine plants.

✴ Location: Signed off the A30 Chard to Crewkerne road or off the A358 Chard to Axminster road.

Further information: www.fordeabbey.co.uk

CHIDEOCK MANOR, BRIDPORT

Dorset has been blessed with many manor houses, one of which is the outstanding and historic Chideock. Set between Bridport and Lyme Regis in beautiful parkland – with an adjoining church – it exudes charm and atmosphere.

The word 'manor' conjures up a vision of feudal England, in which boundaries of allegiance were drawn and rewards of land or favours were granted. The *Oxford Dictionary* describes a 'manor' as an 'English territorial unit', and this is certainly true in the case of the ancient manor of Chideock. Prior to the Norman Conquest, Chideock, or Chidiock as it was then known, belonged to King Alfred, but William the Conqueror seized it within two years. In 1312, Edward II transferred the lands of Chidiock to the first John de Chidiock.

The manor then passed through marriage to the Arundell family, who held it until 1802, when it was purchased by Thomas Weld, whose grandson subsequently married a descendant of the last Sir John de Chidiock. The Welds built the manor house in 1811, and added the Church of Our Lady Queen of Martyrs and St Ignatius in 1874. The church is attached to the house and demonstrates a strong connection with Catholicism in every sense. The Welds lived in the present manor house until the current owners, Howard and Deirdre Coates, moved there in 1996.

When the Coateses arrived, the 5-acre/2-hectare garden was predominantly lawn with hardly any flowerbeds. Few records of the garden layout existed to assist them with the restoration. For this reason, the garden today reflects much of the Coateses' own interpretation of how it might have been.

This is true of the parterre to the rear of the church, the

The Church of Our Lady Queen of Martyrs and St Ignatius rises beside the rear garden and its ornamental pond.

A statue stands by the rose arbour that leads through the Lady Garden.

existence of which Deirdre discovered in outline one frosty morning. It is now recreated in the form of clipped box hedges in-filled with cotton lavender (*Santolina chamaecyparissus*) and a contrasting pea gravel mulch, with standard hawthorn trees standing sentinel at each corner.

During an initial exploration of the property, the Coateses discovered many old architectural pieces, which they have used to enhance the garden. An old mullioned window frame, not thought to belong to the house or church, forms a neat backdrop in the rear garden. Further salvaged relics have been used in the construction of a folly within the Fern Garden, designed to resemble a ruined chapel. Here ferns and bamboos mingle with strategically placed tree stumps, the concept inspired by the stumpery at Prince Charles's garden at Highgrove in Gloucestershire.

The south elevation of the house is adorned with wisteria, which is spectacular when in full bloom. To the rear of the house, a mature *Acer palmatum* dominates an ornamental pond and formal lawn, its ornate leaf form and autumn colour adding greatly to the garden.

To the rear of the church, a path beside a stream, which opens out into a pond, takes you along a lush bog garden planted with massive *Gunnera manicata*, arum lilies (*Zantedeschia aethiopica*), ligularia, rodgersia and hydrangeas. A bridge across the stream leads through an avenue of rose and clematis arches to what Deirdre describes as the Lady Garden and an old thatched summerhouse. Returning to the front of the house, you come to a formal lawned area surrounded by a balustrade, where you can enjoy an exciting view of the lake and parkland beyond.

ABOVE A metallic stag sculpture by George Hider surveys the parterre.
OPPOSITE ABOVE A thatched summerhouse offers a quiet haven.
OPPOSITE BELOW In the parterre outlines of clipped box hedges are filled with twisting shapes of cotton lavender (*Santolina chamae cyparissus*).

✳ Location: Chideock is 2 miles/3 kilometres west of Bridport on the A35. The manor is situated ¼ mile/ 0.4 kilometres north of the village.

No manor house would be complete without its own kitchen garden and orchard. The Coateses are fortunate enough to have two large walled gardens, one for a box-edged vegetable and fruit garden and the other devoted to cider apple trees tended by the Chideock 'cider men'.

THE MILL HOUSE, NETHERBURY

When Michael and Giustina Ryan moved to the Mill House at Netherbury in the heart of rural Dorset, the mill was run down and the adjoining buildings required attention. With some architectural assistance, they have now tastefully transformed the buildings into superb living accommodation, while the garden arranged around them make this venue something very special.

Located off the River Brit, the mill was used to grind corn. In 1893, the traditional waterwheel was replaced with a water-driven turbine, which provided the motive force until 1947, when the mill closed. There remains the potential to use the facility for the generation of electrical power – something that the Ryans are now considering.

Nestling by the side of a stream at the bottom of a valley, with hills rising on either side and the Church of St Mary high on the hillside overlooking the village – a scene reminiscent of the Loire Valley – the garden had considerable potential for development. Having restored the mill, Michael and Giustina applied their talents to creating a spectacular series of interlinking gardens comprising arboretums, streamside walks and walled gardens with terraces.

Later they commissioned garden designers Graham Hopewell and Peggy Curnow to assist with the design of the

BELOW A golden-leaved *Ptelea trifoliata* 'Aurea' adds light to the scene in the terraced garden. The rose on the wall is 'Abraham Darby', with *Geranium pratense* and *G. robustum*, *Cistus* × *purpureus*, *Gladiolus byzantinum*, *Phlomis italica* and white fox-gloves providing additional colour. This area of the garden is also graced with a view of Netherbury's Church of St Mary.
RIGHT Against the backdrop of the Mill House, a magnificent display of red *Penstemon* 'Garnet', with *Papaver orientale* 'Patty's Plum' behind and the contrasting white of *Philadelphus* 'Manteau d'Hermine' to the left.

PREVIOUS PAGES A flowering clematis climbs around a tree trunk beside the millstream in the front garden.
ABOVE The millpond captures the reflections of the surrounding trees.

hard landscaping in some areas. With any commission, there is a delicate balance to be achieved between interpreting the client's ideas and not allowing the designer's own aspirations to dominate. That balance has been achieved here perfectly, and Michael and Giustina's wishes have been faithfully realized.

The garden to the rear of the property slopes down to the millpond, with a series of terraced flower beds. The view from the top of the garden looks beyond the river to the surrounding hillside and St Mary's Church.

To the side of the house, a formal walled garden, created by Graham Hopewell and inspired by Edwardian designers Gertrude Jekyll and Sir Edwin Lutyens, provides a shaded area, with water features adding to the charm. The planting is colourful – two discrete flower borders have been created to display a combination of yellow and white plants in one and blue plants in the other – with an emphasis on fragrance.

A kitchen garden leads along a bank planted with wild flowers and ferns to the first arboretum. There are 5 acres/2 hectares of arboreta in total, planted with a wide variety of trees, including cornus, magnolias, fruit trees, acers, oaks, eucalyptus, conifers, birches, liriodendron, *Nothofagus*, willows and alders. Michael is particularly proud of his Wollemi pine (*Wollemia nobilis*), discovered only recently in New South Wales, Australia, and an unusual plant to be found in this part of the world.

The entrance to the Lutyens-inspired walled garden.

❋ Location: 1 mile/1.6 kilometres south of Beaminster off
the A3066 Beaminster to Bridport road.

MELPLASH COURT, BRIDPORT

As the huge iron gates to Melplash Court open, the view before you is simply magnificent. An avenue lined with chestnut trees leads to one of Dorset's loveliest mansions, made of honey-coloured stone – with a large, round stone dovecote standing near one corner of the house – and set in delightful parkland. As you pass lawns manicured to perfection and falling away to the boundaries, and a landscape interspersed with some of Britain's finest mature trees, it is not difficult to imagine life as it used to be. A horse-drawn carriage would indeed be a more appropriate way to arrive at Melplash than in a modern-day motor car.

Melplash was originally the seat of the de Meleplashe family, the area having been granted to them by Henry II. Since then, like many of Britain's country estates, Melplash has had a succession of prominent owners, and inevitably the estate has been divided up over the years.

The gardens were laid down by Lady Diana Tiarks during the 1950s, when both Melplash Court and Melplash Court Farm belonged to her husband, Peter Tiarks. In September 1984 Timothy Lewis purchased Melplash Court, and over the next twenty years, until his death, he lovingly redesigned the gardens, with the help of Terry Baker of the Botanic Nursery in Atworth, Wiltshire. During those years, much significant new planting took place and the earlier design was completely transformed. Today the gardens are a tribute to an accomplished gardener and plantsman, offering variety and colour at every turn. They are maintained by head gardener Tim Bartlett and his team who, with support from Terry Baker, continue to develop the landscape.

The gardens include a walled garden and croquet lawn with

The immaculate croquet lawn and summer borders.

Grey-green hostas and umbrella-leaved gunnera beside the stream in late spring.

Summer sunlight filters through beech and willow trees in the bog garden.

adjacent borders, which leads into a fern garden surrounded by lime trees. Beyond lies a primula-planted bog garden, approached beneath willow and beech trees underplanted with gunnera and hostas. A small stream and cascade lead to higher ground, where magnolias, acers, hydrangeas and rhododendrons can be seen. Across the stream the garden takes on a more oriental style. A formal kitchen and herb garden provide a fitting exit.

Superbly maintained and sitting comfortably within their historic surroundings, the gardens at Melplash are an absolute joy. The colourful summer borders in shades of blue and white, the magnificent roses, the colours of the bog garden and the specimen trees are but a few of the many qualities that make this truly one of Dorset's most inspirational gardens: a place of character and perfection, which images seem to best describe.

✳ Location: 4 miles/6.4 kilometres north of Bridport on the A3066 Beaminster road.

Further information: the gardens are open by appointment to select groups as well as under the National Gardens Scheme.

A wealth of blooms from *Rosa* 'Iceberg' contrast with the warm stone of Melplash. The roof of the dovecote can be seen on the left.

HORN PARK, BEAMINSTER

The small market town of Beaminster became famed for its association with cognac after local boy Thomas Hine left for France at the age of seventeen in search of his fortune, married into a brandy business in Jarnac, became owner of the company and gave his name to Hine Brandy, now recognized as a connoisseur's vintage cognac. It is also in an area renowned for its country houses, including Mapperton, Parnham, Melplash and Horn Park.

Located in a magnificent hillside setting overlooking some of Dorset's most valued landscape, Horn Park gardens and house sit within some 66 acres/26 hectares of lush farmland and enjoy magnificent panoramic views over the surrounding hillside and to the coast.

The house was designed in 1919 by T. Lawrence Dale, a pupil of Sir Edwin Lutyens, and emulates the style of an Edwardian country house. Built originally for a military man, Colonel Pinney, it is now home to the current owners, David and Angela Ashcroft.

The landscaping of the garden has been largely determined by its location on the side of a hill. It undergoes regular reconstruction, directed by long-serving head gardener Roy Gunning, who has worked for successive owners over some twenty-three years. Having visited Horn Park in 1995, I was reassured on my second visit to note how very little had changed – a testament to Roy Gunning's hand. It was also interesting to observe how some of the landscaping, very new in 1995, had matured and become as established as the house itself.

On either side of the steps leading to the west elevation of the house grows a variegated euonymus and *Dahlia* 'Blackberry Ice'; to the left is a variegated holly tree.

A copper beech spreads its branches over the south lawn with its expansive views.

This is very much a plantsman's garden. Many rare plants and shrubs are displayed in a series of terraces with herbaceous borders and rock and water gardens. A walk through the woodland glade and into the woodland garden seduces you with foliage in autumn and bluebells in spring.

A parterre on the south elevation is interspersed with a series of island beds supported by topiary, box hedges, ornamental shrubs and architectural urns. On the western side, a small stream leads over a bridge and ultimately to a wildflower meadow containing some 164 species, including orchids.

Horn Park is truly a beautiful garden, which lives in harmony with its surroundings, memorable especially for those magnificent views across the Dorset landscape.

✻ Location: 1½ miles/2.4 kilometres north of Beaminster on the A3066 Beaminster to Crewkerne road.

Looking south from the house down to one of the island beds in the south lawn, with the Dorset countryside beyond.

MAPPERTON GARDENS, BEAMINSTER

'The Nation's Finest Manor House': thus *Country Life* described Mapperton in 2006. Set in a delightful valley south-east of Beaminster, an area of outstanding natural beauty, Mapperton is recorded in the Domesday Book as one of Dorset's oldest manors, but most of the current house was built during the sixteenth and seventeenth centuries. Following a succession of owners, it has been home to the Earl and Countess of Sandwich since 1983.

As you arrive through an avenue of tall limes, the Tudor and Jacobean manor with its characteristic twisted finials comes into view, surrounded by honey-coloured Ham stone stable blocks, a dovecote across a courtyard and the adjoining All Saints Church. If you are lucky, you will be greeted by the sight of a sea of white doves waiting to be fed beneath a nearby tree. Immediately, you sense the atmosphere of a bygone time; even the surrounding landscape appears undisturbed and you feel as though history has stepped out to greet you. It is little wonder that such a setting was chosen for the filming of three period films, *Emma*, *Tom Jones* and *Restoration*.

Like all good things, it is best to savour Mapperton slowly, taking in each area of the 15-acre/6-hectare garden as it is revealed, before the senses are fully awakened by a vista that will stay in the mind seemingly for ever.

Entering the gardens at the front of the manor house through imposing stone piers and watched by two lead eagles, you view the courtyard, which in summer is adorned with roses and clematis. A path leads off to the left, to an expansive view of the croquet lawn leading out from the house, surrounded on two sides by high walls supporting a number of trailing and climbing shrubs, including wisteria,

The lower canal garden in autumn.

PREVIOUS PAGES The elegant canal garden with its formal clipped yews.
LEFT ABOVE The daisy *Erigeron karvinskianus* spreads across the steps leading from the Fountain Court to the 1960s orangery. Mounted eagles are very much a feature of the Mapperton statuary.
LEFT BELOW The Italianate Fountain Court.
ABOVE Roses and clematis flower on the double pergola in summer, but now in early autumn it is clothed in splendidly coloured vines, including *Vitis vinifera* 'Purpurea', *V. coignetiae* and *V.* 'Brant'.

solanum, honeysuckle (*Lonicera*) and ceanothus, in addition to magnolias, camellias and roses. The eye drifts towards a stone summerhouse in the far corner, summoning leisurely summer afternoons to mind. With the house to the south and a yew hedge to the east, the extensive lawn area and surrounding walls almost tempt you into believing that this is the limit of the garden. However, when you continue along the path around towards the summerhouse and beyond the yew hedge a very different view is revealed.

The land plunges into a steep, narrow valley in which some 80 feet/24 metres below there are formal gardens with fountains, canals, Italianate features, stone statuary, terraces, a seventeenth-century summerhouse and elegant yew topiary stretching towards the end of the valley, with the Dorset landscape and woodland coming in to meet it on the far side. The vision is breathtaking, especially when accompanied by silence punctuated only with birdsong, and with the light playing across the valley, enhancing the garden design set out many years ago.

There is, in fact, little remaining of the original seventeenth-

The formality of Mapperton's topiary and Fountain Court contrasts with the surrounding Dorset countryside.

century gardens. What we appreciate today are the designs of Ethel Labouchere, who arrived at Mapperton shortly after the First World War and built the formal gardens in the 1920s in memory of her husband. She was a keen watercolour painter and her designs certainly reflect the eye of an artist. After she died in 1955, Mapperton was acquired by South Dorset MP Victor Montagu, Viscount Hinchingbrooke and father of the current owner. He restored the formal gardens, and added a neo-classical orangery in the 1960s and later a wild garden beyond the formal arrangements, thus harmonizing

rise and fall on each side of the pond, linking the orangery and the double pergola. The pergola itself has matured in character to blend with the surroundings, its stone pillars and wooden roof beams entwined with vine, clematis and rose. The golden Ham stone walls make a pleasing backdrop to colourful seasonal plantings and the Mediterranean borders; while the baroque-inspired Fountain Court, surrounded by box and yew, is an especially fine feature of the original garden design. The eye is also drawn to the deep seventeenth-century fishponds or canals, which capture reflections of the summerhouse and the accompanying walls of yew.

It seems that every aspect of the garden has been created with a vision that stands the test of time. Mapperton is without doubt a classic piece of garden design, where the contours of the landscape inspired the concept and provide much of the atmosphere that envelops it today. Add the nation's finest manor house and the vision is complete.

✳ Location: 6 miles/9.6 kilometres north of Bridport off the A35/B3066 and 2 miles/3.2 kilometres south-east of Beaminster off the B3163.
Further information: www.mapperton.com

The owners ask visitors to note that the use of a wide-angle lens can distort the perspective of the original concept.

the established gardens with the rural landscape beyond. The current owners respectfully maintain the original designs of Ethel Labouchere and Victor Montagu, and have allowed the gardens to mature into a timeless masterpiece.

Mapperton remains a garden that inspires and delights the eye at every turn. The carved stone steps are speckled with the pink and white daisy *Erigeron karvinskianus* as they

CORSCOMBE HOUSE, BEAMINSTER

When a lawyer decided that renting a house in Dorset as a retreat from a busy life was not enough and went in search of a more permanent residence, his main criterion was that he 'must be able to develop the garden'. Corscombe House, a former rectory, proved to be the ideal opportunity. It had a garden that was in need of a good deal of care and attention and presented a blank canvas to its prospective owner.

The plan he formulated for the structure of the 2 acres/ 0.8 hectares of garden was based on geometry and symmetry. The garden would have a central east–west axis, with a crossing axis running north to south, thereby creating a series of distinct 'garden rooms' that could be dedicated to varied planting themes. The garden has a hillside setting and was to be designed to complement and enhance the natural beauty of the surrounding landscape.

As you leave the back of the house through a small parterre, the eye focuses on an obelisk standing among fruit trees in the orchard beyond. To reach this, however, you must first pass between six immaculately clipped yews sculpted to form cylinders in the first garden room. Parterre and borders lining the steps to the next room are planted in blues, purples and white.

A set of paved steps takes you through to the next room, which has a reflecting pond, flanked on the right by hot-red, magenta and orange borders which are subject to a continuous planting programme that keeps pace with the seasons'

The Secret Garden, created in 2007, with its central pool, in which stands a scalloped bowl set on an octagonal plinth. Planting here includes *Lavandula × intermedia* 'Grosso', *Santolina pinnata* subsp. *neapolitana* 'Edward Bowles', low-growing holly, Irish juniper, olive trees, lemon trees in pots and roses. The house, church and countryside lie beyond.

LEFT ABOVE Pots of lilies surround the reflecting pond in summer.
LEFT BELOW Flanking the reflecting pond are hot borders filled with shrubs, herbaceous perennials and annuals.

ABOVE A view of the vegetable garden, where *Clematis* 'Perle d'Azur' provides colour and interest among the summer salads and vegetables. Swathes of blue catmint (*Nepeta* 'Six Hills Giant') add contrasting blue.

progress. The adjacent fifteenth-century Church of St Mary overlooks this area of the garden, providing a distinguished 'borrowed landscape'.

A walk through the abundant fruit orchard to the hillside meadow beyond rewards you with spectacular views of the Dorset countryside and the church. The Dorset writer Monica Hutchings climbed the hill behind the house and wrote, 'The view here and from the garden of the old house beside the church is at its best in late spring or early autumn and perhaps best of all just before sunset, when the sky is clear or piled with high cloud and the trees and hills send long shadows across the landscape.'

No visit would be complete without a walk around two other garden rooms: the vegetable garden and the more recently developed and contemporary Secret Garden, fashioned in Persian style with pool and central fountain, lemon trees, lavender and Mediterranean planting.

✽ Location: 3½ miles/5.6 kilometres north-east of Beaminster, signposted off the A356 Dorchester to Crewkerne road.

ABBOTSBURY SUBTROPICAL GARDENS, WEYMOUTH

One of the most amazing gardens in Dorset, Abbotsbury is a subtropical paradise with views of the vast Chesil Bank on Dorset's Jurassic Coast, which is now classed as a World Heritage Site.

The gardens are fortunate in that this coastal area enjoys a higher-than-average amount of sunshine. This, together with the sheltering effect of the surrounding hills and the warming effect of the sea, has helped to create an almost frost-free microclimate in which many tender and exotic plants can happily exist.

The gardens' history began in 1765, when Elizabeth, the 1st Countess of Ilchester, built a large mansion known as Abbotsbury Castle, overlooking the sea. Sadly, the castle no longer exists, but the walled gardens she created as a kitchen garden to support the castle remain, forming the nucleus of the 20-acre/8-hectare site of the subtropical gardens we know today. Successive changes by Elizabeth's descendants followed. In 1808 the 3rd Earl of Ilchester, Henry Fox-Strangway, enclosed surrounding fields to provide woodland. The 4th Earl of Ilchester, William Fox-Strangway, was a diplomat in the Foreign Service and also a leading botanist and expert on the flora of Europe. His wide-ranging travels gave him the opportunity to acquire many new species from such locations as Chile and the Canary Islands, and he introduced new plants to the gardens.

The 5th Lord Ilchester and his wife Mary expanded the

Dahlia 'Bishop of Llandaff' adds bright red accents to this subtropical planting in the Walled Garden.

PREVIOUS PAGES Summer colour in the Walled Garden. Here the lush bold leaves of bananas contrast with mixed delicate colours, the bold red of dahlias and the rich-coloured leaves of the castor oil plant (*Ricinis communis*).

ABOVE Abbotsbury's Himalayan Tea House provides a place to relax during a walk around the gardens. Here the scene through the valley and down to the Sino-Himalayan Glade is a mixture of foliage, texture and colour through all the seasons.

gardens still further and in their care Abbotsbury came to be home to one of England's most comprehensive plant collections: a catalogue printed in 1899 listed some 5,000 plants growing in what was described at the time as a well-tended jungle. The appointment of Joseph Benbow as head gardener in the 1890s was also a significant milestone for Abbotsbury. Coming from the famous La Mortola garden in northern Italy, he would have been familiar with the succulent plants and other exotics from the Mediterranean area introduced to the gardens at this time.

During the period between the two world wars labour was scarce, and the garden became neglected and soon declined beneath weeds and rampant vegetation. During the Second World War, the West Lawn played host to an encampment of the Dorset Light Infantry. It was not until the late 1960s that Lady Teresa Agnew and her first husband, Lord Galway, embarked on a period of restoration, adding a further 3 acres/1.25 hectares between 1982 and 1984. But tragedy came to Abbotsbury in 1987 and again in 1990, when hurricane-force winds and rain struck most of Dorset, destroying many specimen trees and destroying important areas of the gardens.

Under the guidance of the present head gardener and curator, Stephen Griffith, Abbotsbury has picked up its heels again. In 1990 he instigated a ten-year restoration plan, which

The subtropical theme, dominated here by palms, extends around the lily ponds, which are well stocked with golden orfe.

included improving the gardens' infrastructure, redesigning their many features with new planting schemes and introducing many more exotic plants from around the world. Thanks to Stephen's devotion to detail and passion for his plants, and to his team of gardeners, who have tended these gardens for many years, a visit to Abbotsbury has become one of Britain's foremost specialist horticultural experiences.

Take a walk through the Victorian Garden, the West Lawn and up the hillside through the Secret Walk, and visit the viewpoint for a panoramic view of the length of Chesil Bank, stretching from Portland Bill to West Bay at Bridport. Descend into the Sino-Himalayan Glade, where you can see Abbotsbury's collection of large-leaved rhododendrons and

bamboos; and walk along Hydrangea Walk, where you can see *Hydrangea serrata* and *H. macrophylla* varieties, as well as *Styrax japonicus* from Japan. Alongside the stream that runs through the garden grow tree ferns *Dicksonia antarctica* (from Australia) and *D. squarrosa* (New Zealand), and a magnificent display of hostas. Throughout the seasons, the colours and light transform each area of the garden.

Plants like Chusan palm (*Trachycarpus fortunei*) and *Ailanthus altissima* have originated from as far away as China, *Chusquea gigantea* and *Podocarpus salignus* from Chile, and *Cornus capitata* and *Cupressus cashmeriana* from the Himalayas. Plants from New Zealand, Japan, Mexico, USA, Australia, South Africa and many other countries are all represented in these gardens. Abbotsbury's location may well be a landscape setting in Dorset, but its heart is firmly embedded in the faraway, subtropical regions of the world.

ABOVE AND LEFT During October thousands of 1,000-watt halogen 'bulbs' are strategically placed around Abbotsbury, as if the garden is a stage set. With a range of filters — red, blue, green, magenta and natural white — their ghostly light penetrates the depths of the subtropical foliage and creates dynamic effects. Palm trees and ferns look like a distant desert oasis in the dark; and the hillside ruins of St Catherine's Chapel, near the Jurassic Coast viewpoint, are illuminated too, adding depth to the vision. The pathways are lit with candles to guide visitors through their walk. With the sound of birds and animals, the cool night air and a soft breeze, the natural scene is transformed into a truly atmospheric garden experience.

LEFT Glossy-leaved *Trachystemon orientalis* covers the ground
on Fern Island in the Streamside Walk beneath the large fronds of
Dicksonia antarctica.
ABOVE A dramatic example of pieris, as its leathery leaves make the
transition from their springtime red to pink and then creamy yellow,
before returning to their familiar deep green. Like the surrounding
rhododendrons, it enjoys the lime-free soil in this sheltered location.

✽ Location: ¼ mile/0.4 kilometres west of Abbotsbury
village on the B3157 Weymouth to Bridport road.
Further information: www.abbotsbury-tourism.co.uk/
gardens.
Abbotsbury Subtropical Gardens is an affiliated Royal
Horticultural Society garden (entrance for members is free
in winter months) and a member of the Historic Houses
Association.

LANGEBRIDE HOUSE, LONG BREDY

Langebride is the old English spelling for Long Bredy, the name of the secluded village where Langebride House can be found, under steep downs in the Bride Valley. The house, situated on the northern edge of the village, was formerly the rectory for St Peter's Church in the parish of Long Bredy and has been owned for the last thirty years by Mrs Greener and her family. The garden, approximately 3 acres/1.2 hectares, is surrounded by stone walls and is now almost exclusively maintained by Mrs Greener, with some assistance from her family and local sources.

The front of the house is laid to lawn edged with a colourful border containing a selection of spring bulbs and herbaceous plants. A central feature in the lawned area is a magnificent 200-year-old copper beech tree (*Fagus sylvatica* 'Atropurpurea'). This is flanked by two common beech (*Fagus sylvatica*) of similar age and a *Ginkgo biloba*, which dominates the surrounding skyline. Pleached lime trees planted in the 1960s alongside a copper and green tapestry beech hedge provide height and structure, as well as shielding the house from the nearby road.

At the back of the house, the garden becomes a graded hillside that rises to meet the adjacent woodland. The area is planted with a selection of ornamental shrubs; and ascending via a series of carefully placed steps you come to a further elevated lawned area containing an ornamental pond. Through a side gate, more shrubs line the garden wall, with drifts of peonies providing summer colour and alliums dispersed along the border. Mrs Greener and her son have also developed an alpine rockery containing many plants.

A peaceful sunny afternoon in the walled garden.

ABOVE Drifts of peonies provide summer colour in the walled garden.
RIGHT A double magenta peony.
OPPOSITE The lawned front garden with 200-year-old beech trees and in the centre *Ginkgo biloba* and the pink spires of foxgloves in the foreground.

A secondary walled garden is the family kitchen garden, which meets most requirements for the house and which Mrs Greener describes as her 'pride and joy' – a description that should indeed be bestowed upon the garden as a whole.

✳ Location: 8 miles/12.8 kilometres west of Dorchester off the A35 Bridport road.

BROOMHILL, RAMPISHAM

Rampisham in west Dorset is one of the county's most picturesque villages, in one of its most lush, green and well-wooded corners. Church and stream sit comfortably together in the shelter of Toller Down, seemingly miles from anywhere. Visiting this area of beech-lined byroads, manor houses, and cottages with thatched porches and dormer windows is like entering a bygone era and a timeless rural idyll.

Broomhill, the home of Carol and David Parry, is on the outskirts of the village, and their colourful garden hides behind a traditional Dorset cottage. David and Carol moved there in 1972, when Broomhill was considered to be a 2½-acre/1-hectare smallholding. Some fifteen years ago, with the demands of children diminishing, Carol began to indulge

her long-standing interest in gardening, and since then she has turned Broomhill into a 1-acre/0.4 hectare haven of a cottage garden.

You approach the garden via an ornate floral archway of roses, honeysuckle and clematis. A gently sloping lawn takes you past numerous island beds, delicately planted with seasonal annuals, and borders of herbaceous perennials and ornamental shrubs. Clipped box topiary and yew add structure to the garden.

At the lower end of the garden is a large pond, sheltered by adjacent trees, with willows dipping to reach a water surface covered with lilies and a cut pathway circumnavigating it. At one end stand two ornate flamingo sculptures; at the other, a small seat has been provided on which to rest and enjoy the spectacle of the garden. An area has been set aside for growing marginal plants: yellow irises mingle with mimulus

OPPOSITE AND BELOW The gravelled entrance to the cottage passes through an arch clothed with clematis and *Rosa* 'Bantry Bay'.

ABOVE A magnificent vista across the garden.

RIGHT ABOVE A giant pignut (*Carya glabra*) grows beside the pond. On the right the bog garden can be seen sloping down to the pond, which is fed by natural springs.
RIGHT BELOW *Rosa* 'Geranium' (*moyesii* hybrid).

and primulas to form a bracelet around the edge of the pond, while clumps of giant feather grass (*Stipa gigantea*) create movement and sound in the afternoon breeze.

One of Carol's favourite trees, which she won in a raffle some twenty years ago and was 20 inches/50 centimetres high when she planted it, is a Montazuma pine (*Pinus montazumae*) in the lower garden area. Sadly, electricity regulations have meant that the pine has had to be topped, but no doubt it will regain its shape again with time.

As I leave the garden, Carol is planning for September colour, with seedlings already planted in the greenhouse. No doubt she will create further island beds as she continues to enlarge her displays. A cottage garden requires year-round commitment, much attention and enthusiasm, but Broomhill shows what can be achieved: long may it prevail.

✳ Location: 11 miles/17.5 kilometres north-west of Dorchester off the A37 Dorchester to Yeovil road.

THE SECRET GARDEN AT HILFIELD FRIARY

Just a short distance from Minterne Magna lies the Secret Garden of the Society of St Francis, a small woodland garden resting in the shadow of Batcombe Hill on the edge of the Blackmore Vale. Although quite small, it is probably the most peaceful and tranquil garden in this book. It appeared on the television programme *Paradise Gardens* with the late gardening presenter Geoff Hamilton in what turned out to be one of his last appearances.

The garden was owned by the Earl of Sandwich until 1921, when the 9th Earl agreed to let the area to Brother Giles and a group of Franciscans to enable them to set up a home for wayfarers or homeless men travelling about the roads of England in search of work and shelter – a facility that is still offered today. The garden, which began life as a swamp and woodland, was established in the 1950s but fell into neglect, and since 1984 has been transformed into a beautiful rhododendron, magnolia and camellia garden. Because of its seclusion it has become known as the Secret Garden.

The transformation is largely the work of Brother Vincent, a member of the International Camellia Society and of the Rhododendron, Camellia & Magnolia Group within the Royal Horticultural Society. His work with the Society of St Francis has taken him from what was his home in Llandudno in Wales, where his interest in rhododendrons began, to far-off places such as New Zealand. The garden features camellias he has grown from seed collected in China.

The specialist collection of magnolias in the garden

BELOW The palm *Trachycarpus fortunei* in flower.
RIGHT Bamboos at the sheltered edge of the Secret Garden, which looks out on to Batcombe Hill.

Brother Vincent in the Secret Garden, admiring the bloom on a *Rhododendron* 'Rubicon'.

is extremely impressive and includes *M. sargentiana* var. *robusta*, *M.* × *thompsoniana*, *M.* 'Summer Solstice', *M.* 'Apollo', *M.* 'Nimbus', *M. brooklynensis* 'Yellow Bird', *M.* 'Lois', *M.* 'Iolanthe', *M.* 'Star Wars' and *M. denudata*. There is also a selection of rhododendron species and hybrids. The species include *R. thayerianum*, *R. sinogrande*, *R. kesangiae*, *R. calophytum*, *R. sinofalconeri*, *R. auriculatum* and *R. arboreum* in various forms, *R. maccabeanum*, *R. falconeri* and *R. rex* subsp. *fictolacteum*. Loderi hybrids include 'Rubicon', 'Cornish Red' and 'Loder's White', with further hybrids in other parts of the friary garden.

A number of the rhododendrons and other shrubs in the garden have been collected by modern-day plant hunters, namely Peter Cox and his son Kenneth, Roy Lancaster and Bleddyn and Sue Wynn-Jones.

✳ Location: 10 miles/16 kilometres north of Dorchester off the A352 Dorchester to Sherborne road.

A gravel path leading to the Secret Garden.

A statue of St Francis amidst summer colour in the welcoming front garden, where foxgloves and wild flowers mix with cultivated blue geraniums.

SHERBORNE CASTLE

The gardens of Dorset have been associated with many historic events. These and the individuals who have influenced the development of aspects of society through the ages, including architecture, politics, farming, literature and even what has now become known as the English Landscape Garden, have all played their part in Dorset's rich heritage. Sherborne Castle and its magnificent garden – one of Dorset's best eighteenth-century romantic settings – is one such place.

The original castle at Sherborne dates back to the eleventh century. Sir Walter Raleigh erected what he called 'Sherborne Lodge' on the site of a hunting lodge in the deer park of the castle. Unfortunately for Raleigh, he fell out of favour and when accused of treason lost his head on the block, his estate being forfeited to the Crown. In 1617 James I allowed Sir John Digby, soon to become Earl of Bristol, to purchase the castle for £10,000, but it was destroyed during the Civil War and Raleigh's lodge took the name Sherborne Castle. The ruins of the earlier castle are a romantic feature in the 42 acres/ 17 hectares of landscape surrounding the present castle today. The current owner, John Wingfield Digby, is a descendant of the Digby family.

In 1753 Lancelot 'Capability' Brown was commissioned to create the magnificent lake we see today, in the hollow between the old castle and the lodge, in the serpentine style that is his hallmark. He later went on to complete the landscaping of the estate grounds in 1776, although the 1st Earl Digby employed him for further work through to the completion of Pinford Bridge at the end of the lake in 1790.

A tour around the grounds begins at the western end of the 50-acre/20-hectare lake, with a panoramic view along its shoreline past Raleigh's Seat, where it is said Raleigh's

Late afternoon shadows across the sweeping lawns on the southern shore of the lake.

manservant poured a jug of ale over his master on seeing him smoking tobacco for the first time. Over Dinney Bridge, where a crenellated wall has been constructed to divide the old and new castle grounds, the sound of rushing water greets you as you approach Pope's Seat. This seat was named in memory of poet Alexander Pope, who visited in 1724 and particularly

enjoyed a walk to the broken walls of the old castle and the sound of the river near by.

A little further on there is a view across the lake to the southern shore with the boathouse, the castle, the lawns sloping down to the lakeside and the landscape beyond.

As you continue on the north side of the lake, a mock

The walk around the southern shore provides glimpses of the lake and the landscape beyond.

ruined tower comes into sight: a folly constructed in the mid-eighteenth century as part of a scheme to beautify the ruins of the old castle. It is said that Lord Digby liked the then fashionable style of completing a garden vista with a picturesque ruin and incorporated it into his design.

End your explorations with a tranquil lakeside walk back

ABOVE The orangery, seen from across the lawn in front of the castle. In the centre stands a *Ginkgo biloba* which claims the largest girth in the country.

OPPOSITE Autumn colours by the lake. A cedar of Lebanon makes a majestic centrepiece in a planting that includes *Taxodium distichum, Quercus cerris, Metasequoia glyptostroboides, Tilia × europaea* and *Fagus sylvatica.*

to the castle through a superb collection of trees and other plants. Among these are established cedar trees, including specimens of the gigantic cedar of Lebanon (*Cedrus libani*), probably planted *c.*1755 by Henry, 7th Lord Digby, as part of Capability Brown's improvements. There are also perfect examples of ginkgo and *Taxodium*. The walk returns to the southern shore of the lake along rolled gravel paths edged by

well-maintained lawns and borders of herbaceous and other ornamental plants.

There is, of course, much more to see on this magnificent estate. The landscaping of Capability Brown, which surrounds the castle, a deer park and a Gothic cottage all add to the splendour of Sherborne. Today this splendid setting is maintained by head gardener Timothy Stiles and his team. They surely have one of the most satisfying jobs in the county, as they work in sympathy with the ideals of Sherborne Castle's original landscape designer.

✻ Location: ½ mile/0.8 kilometres east of Sherborne, signposted from the A30 and A352.

Further information: www.sherbornecastle.com

Pope's Seat, reflected in the still waters of the lake. The ruins of the
original castle appear through the surrounding trees.

The boathouse on the southern shore, with a Sargent cherry
(*Prunus sargentii*) in its resplendent red autumn colours.

MINTERNE GARDENS

Imagine waking up in the morning, throwing back the curtains and seeing the light haze that covers the lake as the early morning sun begins the evaporation process that will no doubt become tomorrow's rain. From the other side of the valley you can hear the intermittent tap of a woodpecker looking for breakfast. It's early spring and an amorous drake chases his potential bride across the water. This rural scene is as good as you can get in central Dorset, but it is not make-believe: it is Minterne, the home of the Hon. Henry and Mrs Digby.

Take the A352 from the county town of Dorchester towards Cerne Abbas and inscribed on the chalk hillside you will find Dorset's famous symbol of fertility, the Cerne Giant. Soon you will enter Minterne Magna and the land of Thomas Hardy, little changed from his time. He based *The Woodlanders* in the area: Minterne House featured as Great Hintock House in the novel and the oaks pictured in the frontispiece are the very trees still standing today. The timelessness of Minterne House and its gardens makes it a favourite setting for period

OPPOSITE Dappled light and colour in spring beside Minterne's riverside walk.
BELOW The Capability Brown-style landscape that surrounds Minterne.

film and television productions: in 1963, *Tom Jones* was filmed here, starring Albert Finney and Susannah York; and in 1967, Minterne was the location for scenes in John Schlesinger's film adaptation of *Far from the Madding Crowd*, starring Julie Christie, Alan Bates, Peter Finch and Terence Stamp.

The house and the woodland gardens laid out in a horseshoe below it sit in a valley beneath the beautiful chalk hills known as High Stoy and Dogbury, and they have been the home of the Churchill and Digby families for some 350 years. The original house was demolished in 1900 because of dry rot, and replaced with the more eclectic stately home that exists today. The architect of the present house was Leonard Stokes; Sir Edwin Lutyens was one of his early pupils.

In 1768 Admiral Robert Digby, a younger son of the 7th

LEFT In early autumn the landscape across the lake welcomes visitors to the garden and provides a vista of muted colours.

ABOVE The imposing façade of Minterne House, viewed across the lawn from the south.

Baron Digby of Sherborne Castle, bought Minterne and began the landscaping of the 20-acre/8-hectare garden, adding many trees to the valley sides and damming a natural stream to create a lake, cascades and bridges. The second of these bridges was constructed in 1785 and named Lady Eleanor's Bridge after his wife.

Today, as you enter from the north side and look beyond the lake to the valley behind, you see the landscape, arranged in the style of 'Capability' Brown, with traditional trees providing cover for grazing animals and unsuspecting pheasants, of which there are many.

As you approach the gardens from the front of the house, the splendours of the area are revealed. A Japanese cherry avenue with a wonderful display of *Prunus* 'Hokusai' – the plants

were originally brought from Japan in 1905 – provides a vista of pink flowers in spring. Adorning the sides of the banks of the path through the avenue in early spring, narcissi and bluebells emphasize the wonders of the Dorset countryside, while at the top of the bank, many species of trees can be found, including Morinda spruce (*Picea smithiana*), introduced from the Himalayas in 1818, and Weymouth pine (*Pinus strobus*), introduced in the sixteenth century from America and planted here in 1939.

Beyond the end of the Cherry Tree Avenue, you can see the lowest of eleven cascades, the water descending from the valley stream, a tributary of the River Cerne, which continues to the River Frome. Along the bottom of the valley towards Lady Eleanor's Bridge, the planting includes *Rhododendron falconeri*,

and the pocket handkerchief tree (***Davidia involucrata***) behind. Planting for midsummer includes astilbes, iris, hemerocallis, foxgloves, hostas and many others. In autumn, the gardens display a glorious symphony of colour with maples and rare specimen trees.

Through the seasons there is an element of visual surprise around every corner. With the surrounding landscape complementing the scene, Minterne remains one of the most delightful and atmospheric gardens Dorset has to offer.

✳ Location: 2 miles/3.2 kilometres north of Cerne Abbas on A352 Dorchester to Sherborne road.

Further information: www.minterne.co.uk

Foliage beside the path and stream includes that of the Norway maple (*Acer platanoides*) with *A. palmatum* seedlings and evergreen azaleas.

Early spring cherry blossom beside the warm-coloured stonework of Lady Eleanor's Bridge. In the background Chusan palms (*Trachycarpus fortunei*) add a contrasting subtropical note to the scene.

ASHTON FARM, MAIDEN CASTLE

Dorset's connection with history is well documented, and nothing demonstrates this more than Maiden Castle, the largest Iron Age hill fort in Europe. It is thought the construction of the castle began around 3000 BC; artefacts and burial mounds found there date back to the late Stone Age and early Bronze Age. Following the Roman invasion in AD 43 and during the fourth century, a Roman temple was built on the site, the remains of which can be seen today.

In the lee of the castle lies Ashton Farm. The Manor of Ashton was one of the medieval settlements alongside the Winterborne stream, which runs through the garden during most of the year, depending on the amount of rainfall. The farm was once part of a larger country estate that was broken up and sold in lots. Retired farm manager James Shanahan and his artist wife Jenny moved there during 1995 from the Lake District. Jenny says that the property was advertised in 1901 as a 'gentleman's sporting lodge'.

The house was in a very poor state of upkeep. The 2-acre/0.8-hectare grounds around it were overgrown and a hedge of leylandii had to be removed, along with brambles and nettles, before work could start on developing the garden. Then James and Jenny subdivided it into a number of smaller units, all contained within a walled enclosure. They are continuing to extend the garden, pushing it into the surrounding meadow and woodland. Jenny has converted an old outbuilding into a studio called The Chapel and regularly holds exhibitions of her paintings there.

A lawned expanse in the front of the house takes you into an enclosed area with herbaceous borders and the entrance to the

The lawned area in front of the house, which was once a gentleman's sporting lodge.

A sculpture by Jonathan Fry marks the entrance to the walled garden and the beginning of the rill.

walled garden via an arbour. In summer, the fragrance from the many roses adorning the arbour, entrance and borders is memorable: Jenny believes fragrance is an important feature in a garden.

A hanging sculpture, *Noon Seed*, by local artist Jonathan Fry fronts a rill that extends to the back wall and a small seating area. An area set aside as a kitchen garden leads to the white garden, which is surrounded by a clipped yew hedge that Jenny says helps create a microclimate for the plants growing within.

The extended garden runs parallel to the adjacent fields. It includes a small copse referred to as a wildlife haven, and rises through lime trees with sculptured gothic arches. A laburnum-covered arbour leads to the high ground above. Here there is an area ideal for relaxation and alfresco dining: an island garden with a selection of small shrubs and a smoke tree (*Cotinus coggygria*).

As you take your leave of this intriguing garden, you pass a Judas tree (*Cercis siliquastrum*) – unusual as it bears flowers

The rosa mundi: *R. gallica* 'Versicolor'.

The higher garden, complete with a purple-leaved smoke tree (*Cotinus coggygria*) and hostas, is a secluded area that is a haven for wildlife.

on the trunk – that is in full bloom in late spring. A sculpture entitled *Exaltation* and crafted by Jenny's cousin, Bridget McCrum, offers a final farewell.

✻ Location: 3 miles/4.8 kilometres south-west of Dorchester towards Weymouth off the A354.
Further information: www.jennyshanahanpaintings.webeden. co.uk

DOMINEYS YARD, BUCKLAND NEWTON

Buckland Newton is a rural village on the edge of the Dorset Downs, lying under the watershed of the River Piddle flowing south and the River Lydden, whose source is near by and which joins the Dorset Stour further north.

Domineys Yard is home to Mr and Mrs Gueterbock, who were entirely new to gardening when they started their adventure in the spring of 1961. Until then Mr Gueterbock's career in the navy had kept him away from gardening, but a period of 'gardening leave' allowed the planning and hard work at Domineys to begin.

With help and advice from Dorset nurseryman Charlie Marchant of Keepers Hill, Wimborne, the garden project began to take shape. It was a tremendous help that the soil in the area was largely greensand, a good source of nutrients. Despite its location at 500 feet/152 metres on the northern escarpment of the Dorset Downs and overlooking the Blackmore Vale, the 2½-acre/1-hectare garden benefits from an excellent microclimate, as cold air flowing off the hills bypasses the garden and descends to a frost pocket some way below.

The attractive all-season cottage garden is now fully mature and offers a tremendous variety of planting throughout the seasons. Camellias, magnolias, acers, cornus and eucryphia provide a backdrop to beds of perennials and annuals.

A short walk away from the main house and garden is an arboretum, created when Mr Gueterbock retired in 1995. The River Lydden runs through the site – its source only a few hundred yards away – providing interest amongst the alder,

The seventeenth-century cottage and lawn with ornamental shrubs, conifers and a host of perennial plants, photographed in late summer. The bed on the right includes clipped box, *Cornus alternifolia* 'Argentea', *Acer palmatum* 'Eddisbury' and pittosporum.

The Tennis Court Garden with its dry rill. The eastern skyline is enhanced by trees: from left to right, Scots pine (*Pinus sylvestris*), small-leaved lime (*Tilia cordata*) and *Acer platanoides* 'Drummondii'. Other trees and shrubs include pittosporum, *Taxus baccata* 'Fastigiata Aureomarginata', *Azara* 'Variegata', *Taxus* 'Fastigiata', *Camellia* 'Spring Festival', *Magnolia grandiflora* and *Cornus* 'Eddie's White Wonder'.

birch, willow and oak. Other specimen trees and shrubs of the 300 on display include liquidamber, tulip tree (*Liriodendron tulipifera*), crab apples (*Malus sylvestris*) – some of which have been grown from seed – camellias and rhododendrons. Fritillaries and dwarf daffodils add their charms in early spring.

Behind the seventeenth-century thatched house is a patio area fringed with stone-walled beds with numerous planted pots, allowing seasonal plants to be always on display. A feature of this area is a well, some 22 feet/7 metres deep, which has two springs. It goes down to the clay level below the greensand and has never run dry since it was reopened in 1976. The well head is very much in harmony with the house and could be regarded as an original feature, but in fact it was crafted in the workshops of Rugby School by the Gueterbocks' younger son during the mid-1980s.

A formal lawn contrasts with the general informality of the garden in an area that was for some twenty-five years a tennis court. Here, simplicity and a sense of perspective were the aim, achieved with a dry rill. This is surrounded by herbaceous

The well head, with ironwork made by Andrew Gueterbock at the age of fourteen in the Rugby School workshops, adds interest to the raised terrace and surrounding area, and is surrounded by pots of helichrysum, verbena and purple heliotrope.

borders and planted with colourful annuals and perennials, and leads visitors to more enclosed areas, including a small wooded copse where camellias are in flower from December to May and larger trees including pin oak, copper beech, yew and birch provide cover.

Domineys Yard also has a well-stocked kitchen garden. Here, Minarette apples, pears, cherries and vegetables, together with soft fruits and asparagus, live happily together in strip beds, while yew and beech hedging provides shelter from the chill north-easterly winds.

Packed with interest, Domineys Yard is one of those gardens that capture the imagination at every turn: a place in which to stroll, explore and admire.

✽ Location: 11 miles / 18 kilometres south of Sherborne off the A352.

Further information: www.domineys.com

GRANGE COTTAGE, STOURTON CAUNDLE

The Dorset writer Monica Hutchings described the village of Stourton Caundle, on the edge of the Blackmore Vale, as having a number of good farms, farm buildings and charming thatched cottages, and Grange Cottage is one such. Located at the top of Golden Hill, it occupies a privileged, tranquil position and is home to Fleur Miles and her astronomer husband Richard, who moved there in 2002.

Once the preserve of a local wheelwright who doubled as a coffin maker, the property was very run down when they arrived from Cheshire. Local gardener Jenny Gordon had developed the garden some twenty years ago, but now Richard and Fleur have created their own colourful interpretation of an English cottage garden.

The garden is predominately south facing and the soil is what is known locally as cornbrash, a combination of Oxford clay, calcareous grit and coral (the name is derived from the excellent corn land formed by the disintegration of rock) that is free draining and fertile. Richard says that a seam of cornbrash runs north to south across the village, while to the

OPPOSITE AND BELOW Informal planting and box hedging line the path to the cottage door.

A basket arrangement of pinks adds to the cottage garden feel.

Clematis 'Ville de Lyon'.

east the soil is generally of Oxford clay only.

On entering the garden it becomes obvious that much energy has been spent in the sculpting of topiary from yew and box. Two small ponds and a water feature, contained within clipped hedges, add movement to the garden. Borders and informal beds featuring selected peonies, poppies, roses, hellebores and many other flowering plants are awash with colour.

✱ Location: 6 miles/9.6 kilometres south-east of Sherborne off the A3030.

Topiary surrounds the cottage and edges the winding path leading
through the rear garden. *Paeonia lactiflora* 'Bowl of Beauty' makes a
beautiful summer display on the left.

MANOR FARM, STOURTON CAUNDLE

Manor Farm is one of two delightful gardens in the NGS's *Yellow Book* in Stourton Caundle, one of Dorset's most attractive rural villages, in the north-west of the county. (The other is Grange Cottage, page 92.) Manor Farm, in the middle of the village, was previously owned, it is believed, by the children's author Enid Blyton and her husband Kenneth; the farm was the inspiration for her book *Five on Finniston Farm* (1960). For the last forty years, the seventeenth-century farmhouse, barns and garden have been home to Oliver and Sue Simon, who have lovingly turned the garden into the magnificent display that it is today.

A walled garden surrounds the house, providing space for a vegetable garden, a formal lawned area with herbaceous borders and an opportunity to adorn the walls with some very attractive climbing roses. Outside this, a former orchard, which for many years grew cider apples, has been turned into a shrubbery with a further lawned area and herbaceous borders, entered past clipped hedgerows and mature trees. An arbour leads to a gazebo with vines clinging around the frame and trellis – a relaxing place to rest.

There are also three lakes, developed in the 1980s, fed by the Caundle brook and surrounded by willow trees that graciously dip into the water. This area is a wildlife haven where you can enjoy leisurely walks.

It is not surprising that this garden, surrounded by such attractive farm buildings, was the inspiration for a children's novel. The very atmosphere that exudes from it is one of long summer days, childhood adventures and, of course, tea on the lawn with lashings of ginger beer!

In summer an arbour, leading to a gazebo, provides dappled shade with plantings of wisteria, *Rosa* 'New Dawn', *R.* 'Veilchenblau' and *R.* 'Olivia Hill'.

The farmhouse courtyard contains pots of topiary, hostas and traditional summer-flowering displays.

✱ Location: 6 miles/9.6 kilometres east of Sherborne and 4 miles/6.5 kilometres west of Sturminster Newton off the A3030.

RIGHT ABOVE There are a variety of walks amidst the mature trees around the wildlife lakes.

RIGHT BELOW Topiary and climbing plants enhance the entrance to the handsome seventeenth-century farmhouse. *Rosa* 'Compassion' adorns the entrance while *Cistus* × *dansereaui* adds a splash of white under the window.

HOLWORTH FARMHOUSE, WEYMOUTH

Holworth, just inland from Dorset's Jurassic Coast, a World Heritage Site, is a relatively unheard-of place. It is also a long way from the Far East, where Anthony Bush, serving with the Royal Artillery, met his wife Philippa while she was visiting relatives. After they came to Holworth Farmhouse in 1979, Anthony continued his career in the army and later he took up a position as a Queen's Messenger for a further ten years, spending much time away. Now, though, Anthony has been ordained in the Church of England, and they are both very keen gardeners and run a garden landscape and design business, trading as In Arcadia Garden Design.

The Bushes have transformed what used to be an area of rough grass and apple trees to the rear of the farmhouse into a formal lawn and garden area, surrounded by informal borders filled with ornamental shrubs and roses. The 2-acre/ 0.8-hectare garden has been constructed at differing levels to provide pockets of interest in varying styles.

Water plays an important part in the garden's design and has been used on at least three levels. With an eye on water conservation, Anthony has successfully managed to pump water from a lower pond to a fountain outlet at the top of the garden. A series of rills and cascades return it to source, making an important contribution to the garden's ambience.

In the upper section of the garden, an ornate bridge covered with climbing roses leads to a wooden cabin, rather

The house with its borders and formal lawn is surrounded by rolling Dorset countryside where one can enjoy rural walks. A magnificent rambler, *Rosa* 'Francis E. Lester', features to the left of the house while *R*. 'Bonica' and *R*. 'Ballerina' display their gentle pinks in the border.

ABOVE A view from the top pond, with the rill making its way down several levels to a lower pond.

RIGHT ABOVE A wooden bridge leads to a treehouse-like gazebo.
RIGHT BELOW A quiet corner of the garden.

like a treehouse set in the embankment – an ideal place for eating alfresco. Further exploration leads you among mature trees and shrubs to the edge of farmland and stunning views across to the nearby hillside.

Philippa and Anthony are keen to explore opportunities with hydroponics. This is a process where plants are grown with a reliable water supply fed with nutrients, but without soil, allowing them to be left to mature and fruit with the minimum of maintenance and the possibility of extending the natural growing season. The process has been used commercially for a long time, but it is also ideal in a domestic environment for the production of tomatoes, cucumbers, peppers and many other vegetables. It is particularly useful

for small town gardens and greenhouses, where regular attention to plants cannot be guaranteed. It may be the future for gardening in a busy world.

All this now seems a far cry indeed from the times when this house and garden were maintained by the monks from Milton Abbey.

✳ Location: 7 miles / 11 kilometres south-east of Dorchester near Owermoigne and 1 mile / 1.6 kilometres south of the A352.
Further information: www.inarcadia-gardendesign.co.uk

JAPANESE GARDENS, CROSSWAYS

To replicate an authentic Japanese garden requires a considerable amount of specialist knowledge, as the garden will need to represent the cultural, religious and artistic qualities associated with the country. This is something that retired landscape designer and lecturer Geoffrey Northcote and his wife Jean have achieved with distinction. In just ten years they have transformed their front and rear gardens into two fine examples of Japanese garden style.

The area around Crossways has been reclaimed and developed for housing since the Second World War, when it was known as Warmwell Airfield, an RAF fighter base that provided protection to the nearby naval base at Portland. To the rear of the property an area has been set aside with spacious lawns and trees as an RAF Memorial Garden, each tree having been planted in tribute to a pilot who lost his life during the conflict.

The front open-plan garden alongside the driveway features a raised bed in the form of a turtle, related to the form of the Kame Shima (Turtle Island), a rock and pine composition found in many Japanese gardens. The island sits amid a sea of rounded Chesil pebbles and can be explored by circular stepping stones. In Japanese culture, a turtle is seen as a symbol of longevity and old age. Geoffrey and Jean affectionately refer to theirs as their 'one foot in the grave'. This garden has a colour scheme of yellow, green and blue.

Geoffrey is a trained designer and ceramicist – he has his own British ceramic mark – and around the garden his ability as an artist can be admired. On entering the porch, you see a magnificent mural depicting a Sansui Japanese landscape

In the rear garden, designed in dry landscape style, the river of life is depicted in white gravel.

ABOVE Extensive Japanese-style planting lines the river.
OPPOSITE The river of life continues through the garden and exits under the moon-waves bridge.

showing the *Path of Enlightenment and Kyoto's Golden Pavilion of Kin Kanji*, featuring Mount Fuji in the background, with the Dragon Gate Waterfall to the side. It is said in Japanese mythology that when carp achieve safe passage of the waterfall they turn into dragons. In modern Japan, 'carp badges' are awarded to children for their achievements in examinations.

A green lawn-carpeted passageway leads you past the second of Geoffrey's artistic examples: his millennium *Moon Gate Mural*, which introduces a new contrasting red/green colour scheme. Appropriate Japanese imagery replaces Chinese forms in a traditional willow-pattern plate composition.

The second garden to the rear of the house is designed in *karesansui* (the word means 'withered mountain water') or small dry landscape style. An eternal water source and river, symbolized in white gravel, issues from a 'sanson three-rock group', through a rock 'dragon gate', down the 'torrents of youth' with a 'carp stone', under the 'bridge of adolescence', and past the 'lamp of knowledge', a 'treasure ship stone' of middle age and the 'turtle of old age'. The 'river of life' finally disappears under a 'moon-waves bridge' into a 'sea of oblivion' to the next-door neighbour's garden via a concealed mirror.

The garden includes hand-carved red granite lanterns and stone features such as a *goju no tou* or pagoda, a white marble gravel river with contrasting red border gravel and a *tobi-ishi* stepping-stone oval walkabout. Calming horizontal

The bridge of adolescence, with the *rankei toro* lantern in the foreground, symbolizing the lamp of knowledge.

The *kasuga toro* lantern.

layers and lines are provided not only by the landscaping but also by several traditional timber constructions with red foreground railings and by the *torii* (gateway) leading to the Memorial Garden. All achieve a sense of tranquillity.

A rich variety of foliage, including that of acers, cordylines and palms, as well as a splendid tapestry of flowers, has been integrated into the design. Geoffrey has modified the neutral soil, lying over a sub-base of lime, with additional topsoil and compost to achieve a tolerant and acidic soil more suitable for the acid-loving plants such as rhododendrons and azaleas appropriate to the Japanese style. Between them the rear

garden of 26 × 36 feet/8 × 11 metres and the front garden 36 × 38 feet/11 × 11.5 metres contain 330 different plant species.

Born of studious research into the symbology of rock formations and colours and 2,000 years of Japanese history and culture, the miniaturized landscape offers visitors an atmospheric experience, strongly contrasting with its Dorset surroundings.

✳ Location: 6 miles/9.6 kilometres east of Dorchester, close to Moreton on the B3390.

Symbolic stone features beside the river of life.

HILLTOP, WOODVILLE, STOUR PROVOST

As the month of August gently slips away, dahlias provide an outstanding display of colour in many Dorset gardens, and the garden at Hilltop is no exception. Summer colour is the hallmark of this garden, which Josse and Brian Emerson have developed over twenty years.

Having purchased the 250-year-old thatched cottage in rural north Dorset, Josse and Brian wanted to create a garden to complement the surrounding landscape. At the edge of this south-facing garden of ⅓ acres/0.13 hectares you are treated to magnificent views of the tranquil Blackmore Vale, the area of Dorset much featured in Thomas Hardy's novels and which remains much as then, truly the real Dorset.

Initially, they purchased the property as a 'Dorset strip', an area of farming usually at the top of an escarpment or slope. They then purchased a further adjacent 'strip' from a local farmer and the construction of Hilltop's garden began. First, though, they had to remove and extend the boundary hedges.

BELOW *Dahlia* 'Procyon'.
RIGHT An exuberant planting of dahlias in front of the 250-year-old thatched cottage.

A meandering path takes you past a riot of colour provided by the dahlia collection, which includes *D.* 'Raffles', *D.* 'Silver Years' and *D.* 'Stolze von Berlin'.

Much of the soil was unworkable, the ground having been scalped by continuous farming and the grazing of cows, and they had to import topsoil.

Today, as you enter Hilltop you are greeted by a riot of contrasting colour and scent from numerous flowers in borders and hanging baskets. Unusual annuals and perennials mingle with the traditional phlox, roses, clematis, sweet peas, asters and, of course, those wonderful dahlias.

The garden is a haven for wildlife. Butterflies and bees enjoy the fragrance and colour, while swallows and house martins swoop above, looking down on what must be a delightful view. A meandering pathway takes you past a wildlife pond.

Central to the garden is a massive oak, thought to be the same age as the cottage. Its spreading branches provide shade, under which visitors can enjoy the silence, the view and Josse's homemade cakes. Also around the oak is an area where wooden sculpture and garden implements provide a corner of interest.

Beside the cottage on the eastern side of the garden, Josse and Brian run a small nursery in which you can purchase many of the plants seen in the garden, and garden stone art by Paul Harvey of Whitchurch in the neighbouring county of Hampshire.

Hilltop is an away-from-it-all garden where colour, fragrance and rural views accompany the sound of silence; perhaps this is the rural ideal to which many of us aspire. Here the Emersons have certainly realized their dream, and now they enjoy and share with others the wonderful atmosphere and sights they have created.

Phlox (left) and *Dahlia* 'Golden Sceptre' (right) at the entrance to the
arch that shades the walkway leading to the nursery from the main
garden.

✳ Location: 5 miles/8 kilometres north of Sturminster
Newton near the village of Stour Provost off the B3092.

Further information: www.hilltopgarden.co.uk

COOMBE COTTAGE, SHILLINGSTONE

On the River Stour's journey to the sea, the Stour Valley opens out and the river runs under the hills, passing the village of Shillingstone on its way towards Blandford Forum. The village, which has a fine church with Norman connections and a beautifully carved village cross, was once famous in Dorset for its maypole dancing and for a warning to bell ringers 'not to drink or wear spurs on duty'. The village industry was gathering moss, and up the hills behind the village there is evidence of the drove roads used to send the moss to Covent Garden for use as packing and decoration. The surrounding chalk downland is wonderful for wildlife and wild flowers, and still bears the scars of another former village industry, the chalk pits where lime was produced.

Many of the distinguished houses and cottages within the village are typical of this area of Dorset, and none more so than Coombe Cottage, now home to Mike and Jennie Adams. Jennie has lived in Shillingstone most of her life and Mike for twenty-eight years, and they have been creating the interesting and well-maintained garden together since 1987.

The garden, which covers ⅓ acre/0.13 hectares, can be described as a plantsman's garden, delineated by walls and hedges of beech, box, lonicera and yew. Arbours provide a focus for garden views, while an ornate Romany open-lot wagon supplies additional interest.

Mike, who has a doctorate in biology and is a keen entomologist, has spent much time exploring the Andes in search of rare species of butterfly that can be found only at

A colourful subtropical planting beside the planthouse: orange ginger lily (*Hedychium coccineum* 'Tara') and *Phygelius × rectus* 'Winchester Fanfare' at top left, with a tall variety of scarlet sage (*Salvia splendens*) and pale purple *Salvia involucrata* in the foreground.

Left to right: daisy *Buphthalmum salicifolium*, *Canna* 'Striata', *Dahlia* 'David Howard', purple sage (*Salvia officinalis* 'Purpurascens') and, at the back, *Canna altensteinii*.

RIGHT ABOVE A traditional Romany open-lot wagon.
RIGHT BELOW An interesting combination of the ornamental purple filbert (*Corylus maxima* 'Purpurea'), the grass *Molinia caerulea* subsp. *arundinacea*, paddle-leaved *Canna* 'Mystique' and spiky *Yucca gloriosa* 'Variegata'.

high altitude. His travels, especially those through Venezuela and Colombia, have encouraged an interest in the more exotic subtropical plants, many of which are to be found in the garden. For twenty-two years, he has experimented with more than 1,500 species and cultivars, a number of which he has grown from seed or cuttings.

His adventures in search of butterflies have trained his eye in colour and boldness of planting, relying on foliage, form and hot colours. However, the garden also demonstrates Jennie's preference for pastels and whites. The styles harmonize well and combine to lend a cottagey feel to the garden.

Towards the centre of the garden, in a gently raised area, there is rustic screening with arches covered in roses, clematis, claret vine (*Vitis vinifera* 'Purpurea') and wisteria. Here the borders include varieties of hardy geraniums, aquilegia, astrantia, campanula, pulmonaria and brunnera.

In 2001, the Adamses constructed a large Victorian planthouse in which Mike can indulge his passion for subtropical plants. Here he can overwinter many of his collection of cannas, salvias and palms, while the building itself assists in providing winter shelter for the Japanese banana (*Musa basjoo*) outside. Alongside the greenhouse are further plantings of bananas, cannas, dahlias and hedychium, giving something of a jungle feel to this garden of colour, variety and surprise.

✱ Location: 5 miles/8 kilometres north-west of Blandford Forum on the main A357 road to Sturminster Newton.

THE FERNS,
EAST BURTON

From East Burton meadowland runs gently down to the River Frome and Woolbridge Manor, where Tess in Thomas Hardy's *Tess of the D'Urbervilles* spent her wedding night. On the southern side, the village is split in two by the mainline London-to-Weymouth railway. East Burton began to change in the late 1950s, when Britain's quest for cheaper energy brought research into fast breeder reactors to nearby Winfrith Heath and the formation of the United Kingdom Atomic Energy Authority, and development of the area continues today as East Burton stretches its legs southwards.

John and Jill Redfern moved into the village in 1982, and in 2000 they built an attractive home further down the road. Behind it they have created an almost secret garden of ⅓ acre/0.13 hectares, clearly maintained with craftsman-like care.

An irregular-shaped lawn, perfectly manicured with tangential curves and edges, provides an opportunity for deep borders filled with flowers, ornamental shrubs and small trees, which stretch to the boundary edge. The borders are awash with colour, and obelisk planters supporting climbing

BELOW A bench under a mature apple tree offers a place to sit and enjoy the copious planting that surrounds the lawn.
RIGHT A stone archway separates the kitchen garden from the lawned area and carries the eye through to the borders beyond.

Against a backdrop of apple trees, the planting here includes yellow *Ligularia przewalskii* and a white geranium.

plants such as clematis have introduced an additional vertical element.

Jill claims design rights to this part of the garden, but she has allowed her husband John to indulge in a little nostalgia for his previous employment as a carpenter at Furzebrook with the English China Clay Company by reproducing a mine entrance, complete with a genuine underground clay skip.

Passing the mine entrance, which is overhung with trees, you come to a small stream, with ferns embedded along its banks. This runs along the back of the garden and adds the soft sound of running water to an otherwise quiet area.

John lays claim to the front garden, where he has used broken slate and strategically placed stones to enhance a display of ornamental grasses and a selection of ground-covering junipers.

This is one of those private gardens within the NGS scheme that, being a home and hobby, has become a tribute to its creators, lovingly tended and providing much enjoyment to both owners and the visitors with whom it is shared.

✳ Location: 1 mile/1.6 kilometres from Wool off the A352.

In the front garden, plants include spruce grasses and ground-
covering junipers, while local stones provide a link to the Dorset
landscape.

WATENDLATH, BERE REGIS

Why 'Watendlath'? Peter Whittaker, the owner of the house, enthusiastically replies that it is the name of a picturesque hamlet in the Cumbrian mountains where he and his wife Carole have celebrated many happy occasions, including their thirtieth wedding anniversary. The village of Bere Regis in Dorset, where the garden of Watendlath is located, may not quite compete with the scenery of the Lake District, but it has its own gentle beauty and a wealth of literary and agricultural history.

The garden Peter and Carole Whittaker have created is within view of Woodbury Hill, famed for its annual fair, which took place there until the 1950s. The fair was known for its bare-knuckle fighting, bawdy penny peep shows and oriental carpet salesmen from London and as a gathering place for local agricultural workers. Thomas Hardy referred to it as Greenhill in his novel *Far From the Madding Crowd*.

Bere Regis, or Kingsbere, as Hardy called it, was the setting together with Dorchester (Casterbridge) and Wool (Wellbridge) for *Tess of the D'Urbervilles*, the main character of which was based on the Turberville family, who once lived in Bere Regis.

The village also played an important part in the agricultural revolution and riots of 1830, when agricultural workers from there and surrounding farms, disaffected with their pay and conditions, sought to create a trade union. Their efforts culminated in the deportation of six labourers from Tolpuddle to Australia and the eventual foundation of a union in 1872.

Peter, a fire safety manager with the Dorset Fire Brigade, and Carole moved to Bere Regis in 1999 and have progressively

A profusion of summer colour in the borders, with the slopes of historic Woodbury Hill in the background.

Varieties of *Acer palmatum* are shielded from windburn in this mini courtyard Japanese garden, while bamboo, *Ophiopogon planiscapus* 'Nigrescens' with its almost black, strap-shaped leaves and nasturtium (*Tropaeolum*) complete the picture.

The rose garden in summer, where a variety of David Austin roses are underplanted with nepeta, echium and *Tiarella* 'Spring Symphony', surrounded by lavender and box.

created a garden of densely packed herbaceous borders, island beds, and rose and vegetable beds. In 2000 they added a small pond, backed by an enormous gunnera, where Peter has made an artificial bog garden. The pond is planted with water lilies, iris and reeds, while a Japanese-style waterfall adds gentle sound and movement to the garden. Some ⅓ acre/0.13 hectares in size, the garden attracts a variety of wildlife.

Much of the soil around Bere Regis is chalky, and Peter says the soil in the front garden was very shallow and needed

improvement in order to grow the plants we see today. To the rear the chalk is deeper down, but he still finds it difficult to grow roses and prefers to plant them in sunken pots.

The Whittakers have overcome the problem of plants being susceptible to windburn in the exposed location under Woodbury Hill by creating an enclosed Japanese courtyard garden, shielded by a willow screen. This is planted with varieties of *Acer palmatum*, bamboo (*Arundinaria*), *Ophiopogon planiscapus* 'Nigrescens' and nasturtium (*Tropaeolum*), which,

The spectacular white garden with cascading sweet peas and white dahlias. This area also includes a large number of annuals and perennials, including hemerocallis, liatris and phlox.

combined with ferns and a decorative slate, make an attractive secluded area.

Carole has created a white garden, planted profusely with dahlias, sweet peas, lupins, sweet rocket, chrysanthemums, liatris and nicotiana, backed with *Rosa* 'Rambling Rector'.

During July and August the garden is awash with densely packed dahlias, including their favourite, *Dahlia* 'Bishop of Llandaff', which provides a spectacular show.

Keen to provide a garden of interest to all members of the family, Peter and Carole have chickens in a small pen at the rear of the garden. On open days, they place small animal statues around the garden to encourage children to explore its deeper recesses and in doing so experience lots of different scents and textures.

Recent additions to the garden include raised beds for vegetables, which are planted in geometric patterns to show off colour and form, creating a potager effect. Soft fruits grow here in summer, and there is a heavy-cropping 'Peregrine' peach tree that thrives in the alkaline soil.

✱ Location: 13 miles/21 kilometres east of Dorchester off the A35.

SHUTE FARM, DONHEAD ST MARY

Shute Farm would normally be considered to be in the county of Wiltshire, but the close proximity of Donhead St Mary to Shaftesbury in the north of Dorset has allowed the NGS to include the farm in the *Yellow Book* as a Dorset garden.

James and Olivia Douglas have lived here since 1991, painstakingly changing and developing the grounds to form today's charming garden. Surrounded by their alpacas, rare breeds of chickens and hives of bees, it feels closely linked to nature and the surrounding Wiltshire/Dorset landscape.

A water source running beneath the road forms a stream as it enters the 1½-acre/0.6-hectare garden, with cascades that widen to provide water for a large pond. Two smaller ponds below are also fed from this source and all form a magnificent sight with the garden. The central pond with its artificial island provides a safe refuge for nesting ducks; the edges are planted with ornamental shrubs and backed by Himalayan birch trees (*Betula utilis*).

The gardens surrounding the house are planted in cottage garden style with formal lawned areas encompassed by informally planted herbaceous borders and shrubberies. Fruit cages and a kitchen garden yield provisions for the house.

Fields adjoining the rear of the property provide grazing for the alpacas and freedom for the chickens, with a magnificent view of the Donheads. The edge of the field and lower garden are a dedicated wildflower area that leads to the two smaller ponds.

A walk back to the main garden takes you through a wooded glade planted with foxgloves, iris, hostas and arum lilies.

Delicate planting along the stream and reflections in the small pond make this a colourful yet relaxing corner. The landscape surrounding Shute Farm is always apparent; a magnificent view of the Donheads can be seen in the background.

The thatched cottage sits comfortably in this garden, looking out on to lawn and a selection of trees, shrubs and borders that include drumstick primulas and variegated iris.

RIGHT ABOVE A safe haven for ducks in the central pond, backed by Himalayan birch (*Betula utilis*) and the rolling countryside beyond.
RIGHT BELOW LEFT A path from the wildlife pond leads through the woodland glade, where iris and arum lilies (*Zantedeschia aethiopica*) enjoy the dappled shade.
BELOW RIGHT Water enters the garden via a natural spring to form this stream and cascade.

A garden with this degree of complexity requires year-round maintenance. To this end, James and Olivia are aided by Jean Lucas, who on completion of her horticultural training spent some time working at Highgrove, in Gloucestershire. Now settled on the Wiltshire/Dorset border, she and her helpers nurture both the garden and animals.

With the surrounding landscape and views of the church tower from the garden, Shute Farm's cottage garden is a true rural idyll and about as close to nature as you can get.

✱ Location: 3½ miles/5.6 kilometres north-east of Shaftesbury off the A350.

KNITSON OLD FARMHOUSE, SWANAGE

Farming in the British Isles has never been the easiest way to make a living, and this is no less true of farming in the Isle of Purbeck. To quote Rachel Helfer: 'Purbeck is a very difficult place for gardening or farming. Very long droughts, high cruel winds, and then soggy periods' – and that is just in August. Nevertheless, Mark and Rachel Helfer have lived, worked, farmed and gardened here at Knitson Farm since 1956.

When Mark and Rachel bought the house, the garden was an abandoned kitchen garden, a wilderness of nettles and docks with no lawn or decorative planting. Today it is a 1-acre/0.4-hectare garden with seasonal flowers, herbaceous borders and a lawn levelled to provide a discreet seating area surrounded by raised beds, climbers and shrubs. Sloping paths lead through to a lower garden area, and the views across the downland – the Isle of Purbeck is one of Dorset's most delightful locations, and the garden is set under the whaleback of Nine Barrow Down – are framed through an ornate Moon Arch, constructed from local Purbeck stone by Rachel's daughter, Becca, and her husband, Bruno.

Near the popular seaside town of Swanage and the ruins of Corfe Castle, Knitson Farm has over the years uncovered many artefacts of a bygone age, which Mark and Rachel have used to enhance the garden design. Stone gateposts have been adapted as steps; old sinks produced in local quarries are now used as planters, to great effect; and the remnants of Roman occupation and corner stones that once were used as

Looking back through the Moon Arch towards the old farmhouse and the colourful borders.

131

Borders and stone artefacts lead the eye towards spectacular views through the Moon Arch and to the Purbeck landscape to the west. The plants have been collected by Rachel over more than fifty years and many are from self-sown seedlings.

boundary markers for the Studland estates have all been put to good use.

The framework of the garden is important to Rachel. She finds real joy in 'fiddling' in the flower garden and fills empty spaces with plants that can be grown easily, complement the backdrop and provide colour where there is a shortage. Star performers in the garden have been the clematis and montbretia, which welcome you to the front of the old farmhouse, and *Rosa* 'Blush Noisette', which clings to the south and north walls.

Not to be missed is the organic fruit and vegetable garden. This grows seasonal vegetables year round and some twenty varieties of fruit, from cobnuts to kiwis. Knitson thus has a high degree of self-sufficiency, which is important to Rachel, who is a committed permaculturist.

The garden at Knitson Old Farmhouse is a magnificent contribution to this living earth, a treasure trove of history and colour, all displayed with character and a sense of fun.

✳ Location: 1 mile/1.6 kilometres north-west of Swanage and 3 miles/5 east of Corfe Castle off the A351.

The domed tree is *Elaeagnus* × *ebbingei*. Also in view are
Alstroemeria aurea and *A.* 'Princess Victoria', a white semi-cactus
dahlia and in the foreground a pink spiraea.

CORFE BARN, BROADSTONE

Located on the edge of heathland that stretches towards the shores of Poole Harbour, Corfe Barn was built *c*.1728. Later it became part of a lavender farm, established in the early 1900s when some 60 acres/25 hectares of a dairy and poultry farm were given over to the production of lavender for conversion into perfume at nearby Broadstone. The tale of the ghost of the lavender lady originates from this time: it is said that a pretty young woman lost her child in a nearby swamp and returns to the area, presumably in search of the child.

Corfe Barn is now the home of John McDavid, a retired international banker, and his wife Kathleen, who moved to this part of Dorset in 1987, having spent much of their time in West Africa. Kathleen, who is the inspiration behind the garden, has had a passion for gardening since she was a small girl, when her father gave her a packet of seeds and a small patch of the garden in which to cultivate them. When John married her in Sierra Leone, she set about creating a garden in what was known as a 'no grow' area. Her efforts were eminently successful and her skills eventually travelled with her to Dorset. Since the McDavids arrived, they have returned the area around the barn to cultivation and created a colourful and imaginative garden.

The variety of plants and mixed foliage resulting from careful planting are stunning features throughout the year. As you move around the three-level site, the eye is constantly drawn to many pockets of colour and interest. Kathleen has a particular passion for roses, clematis and pinks, which are well represented in the garden. There are six species of eucalyptus

Corfe Barn was once part of a lavender farm, and the stone birdbath is said to have been made from the stone that crushed the lavender to produce oil.

Rosa 'Wedding Day' puts on a splendid display in the higher part of the garden.

tree and many interesting flowering trees and shrubs within the ⅔ acre/0.27-hectare site. A particular feature is the old lavender farm walls, which form an interesting link to the garden's past and add character.

John has provided the hard landscaping within the garden, using recycled material from the old farm and redundant trees to produce wooden seating, arbours and arches. Of particular interest is the large stone birdbath beside the fishpond, which is said to be made of the stone that crushed the lavender harvest in order to extract the oil. There is also a small stream in the garden and a constant supply of natural spring water from which the plants clearly benefit.

✱ Location: 1 mile/1.6 kilometres west of Broadstone town centre, between Wimborne Minster and Poole off the B3074.

A eucalyptus tree with its pale bark makes a stunning centrepiece.

CANFORD SCHOOL ARBORETUM, WIMBORNE MINSTER

Canford School stands in a magnificent parkland setting beside the River Stour on the outskirts of Wimborne Minster. Its origins as a manor can be traced back to Saxon times, and ownership has passed through the Earls of Salisbury and, as part of the Duchy of Lancaster, the Crown. Today only the Norman church and the fourteenth-century John of Gaunt's kitchen survive from those times.

The main school building was designed by Edward Blore and later by Sir Charles Barry in the early and mid-nineteenth century, and is Grade I listed. Sir Charles Barry's design includes a number of features reminiscent of the Houses of Parliament, for which the architect is renowned. It was built for Sir John Guest and his family, who were major landowners in the area, their estate encompassing much of the heathland between Poole and Wimborne. The school was founded at the manor in 1923.

Within the parkland is a rich 250-acre/101-hectare arboretum dating from Victorian times, which makes a splendid backdrop to the school. The unique and varied collection provides much interest and colour throughout the seasons, especially in autumn.

Exceptional among the trees is a great sweet chestnut (*Castanea sativa*) with such an enormous girth it has been

OPPOSITE The gatehouse entrance and porter's house reflected in the millstream off the River Stour in early autumn.
BELOW Canford's famous avenue of sweet chestnuts (*Castanea sativa*), seen here in early morning autumn mist.

Canford's parkland setting in autumn, with myriad displays of
hornbeam (*Carpinus betulus*), Persian ironwood (*Parrotia persica*)
and red oak (*Quercus rubra*).

listed in the *Guinness Book of Records*. Near the golf course lie
the remains of another ancient Canford tree, the Mountjoy
oak, which became the symbol of Canford and appears on the
arms of the school. A number of trees have survived since
the seventeenth century, and others were planted by Lord
and Lady Wimborne in the 1800s, including specimens of
blue Atlas cedar (*Cedrus atlantica* Glauca Group), tulip trees
(*Liriodendron tulipifera*), oak (*Quercus*) and lime (*Tilia*).

There is also a very fine dawn redwood (*Metasequoia
glyptostroboides*), planted in 1960. The tallest tree in the
arboretum is a wellingtonia (*Sequoiadendron giganteum*),
standing at over 100 feet/30 metres and providing a
landmark in the area. One of the later additions is a wollemi
pine (*Wollemia nobilis*), which was discovered in Australia as
recently as 1994.

The arboretum hosts two National Plant Collections as part
of the scheme run by Plant Heritage (formerly the National
Council for the Conservation of Plants and Gardens). One
collection is of the katsura tree (*Cercidiphyllum japonicum*),
notable for its blaze of autumn colour and a smell of burnt
sugar as the leaves begin to fall. The second is of the walnut
(*Juglans*), known for the quality of its timber and, of course,
its edible fruits.

Since the school began in 1923, the arboretum has been
maintained and expanded. Between 1935 and 1982, Hillier's
Nursery of Winchester supplied many new trees and assisted

A red oak (*Quercus rubra*) with its magnificent autumn foliage in front of the school.

with surveys and identification. In 1972 Roy Lancaster and P.H. Gardner surveyed and checked the identity of all the trees. This diligent care is continued today by the arboretum staff, Andrew Beale and Chris Bartlett, who publish *The Arboretum Guide* in order to assist a greater understanding and appreciation of the trees surrounding the school.

Moortown Coppice, to the south of the golf course, is also an interesting area, of oak woodland containing hazel and bluebell. It has been recognized as a Site of Nature Conservation Interest (SNCI) by the Dorset Wildlife Trust, because of the existence of a number of important flora species.

✱ Location: South of Wimborne off the A349 in the village of Canford Magna.

Further information: www.canford.com

Although the arboretum is not generally open to the public, the arboretum team give guided walks by appointment and are always willing to share their knowledge to promote interest and appreciation of the trees and landscape surrounding the school.

ABOVE The outstretched limbs of an English oak (*Quercus robur*) against the snow-covered Higher Park and the headmaster's house.
RIGHT ABOVE The ancient buttress of the only surviving great sweet chestnut (*Castanea sativa*). There were once six of these great trees within the Canford estate. They are illustrated in Hutchins' *History of Dorset* (1802); manorial records trace them back to around 1100, and they were mentioned in the Domesday Book of 1086. This remaining example is recorded in the *Guinness Book of Records* as one of the largest girthed trees in Britain.
RIGHT BELOW The silhouette of a lime tree (*Tilia × europaea*) casts winter shadows across the parkland. On the far right can be glimpsed the avenue of sweet chestnut (*Castanea sativa*).

KNOLL GARDENS, HAMPRESTON

Knoll Gardens is one of Dorset's horticultural success stories, a carrot field that is now an award-winning and internationally known centre for an extensive range of ornamental grasses.

The original planting of the carrot field and semi-woodland at Stapehill, not far from the market town of Wimborne Minster, was undertaken in the early 1970s by John May and his wife. The former market garden was called The Knoll, which the Mays developed into a nursery specializing in Australasian plants; many of the fine trees that can be seen today, including the eucalyptus, are from their selective plantings. Through their hard work and enthusiasm, the collection of plants increased and the garden became known as Wimborne Botanic Garden.

In 1988, the year when the garden was first shown on BBC television's *Gardeners' World*, the garden changed hands and was renamed Knoll Gardens, reflecting the original name. The new owners introduced the formal gardens and water features, which are still enjoyed today.

In 1994, the 4-acre/1.5-hectare gardens became the responsibility of Neil Lucas and John and Janet Flude. Bringing with them many interesting and unusual plants from their own collections, this highly accomplished team carried out major refurbishment. They established National Plant Collections of deciduous ceanothus, phygelius and fountain grasses (*Pennisetum*) and introduced a wide variety of hardy perennials.

Through successive years of development and Neil's many gold medals, including eight consecutive gold awards at the Royal Horticultural Society's Chelsea Flower Show, Knoll

Morning light adorns the New Mill End borders. In the foreground are red *Persicaria* and on the right *Cortaderia selloana* 'Evita'.

A shaded resting place in front of the Decennium Border.

Seed heads of *Pennisetum alopecuroides* 'Red Head' and plumes of *Cortaderia selloana* 'Monstrosa', captured in morning light.

Gardens has become a leading specialist nursery and show garden.

An early morning walk around the garden in October is a most rewarding experience. The autumn mist clings to the branches of spindle trees (*Euonymus latifolius* and *E. europaeus*) and hugs the wands of the many species and varieties of *Pennisetum*, *Stipa* and *Miscanthus*. The colours and tones are muted in the morning light, giving the garden a magical atmosphere. Back lighting enhances the delicate texture of the grasses as they gently sway in a light breeze, and at every turn in the path a new vision of the colours of the changing season presents itself.

In the Decennium Border, planted in what Neil describes as a naturalistic style, the subtle colour mixtures of late summer and early autumn combine with swathes of *Miscanthus sinensis* 'Flamingo' and *M. s.* 'Ferner Osten', harmonizing with the colourful foliage of surrounding ornamental shrubs. Here, the spectacular display of ornamental grasses provides interest and texture through the winter and into March, when they are cut down to allow another year's growth.

Neil has used his experience of landscape design throughout the garden to display the planting to its best effect by using a variety of mulches, gravel and bark and introducing fallen timber boughs to enhance the display.

Adjacent to the water garden and its magnificent waterfalls, a raised Dragon Garden has been created, with a central pond in which sits a dragon sculpture, *Guardian of the Garden*. This

The Dragon Pond in early autumn.

commissioned work was sculpted by Susan Ford and installed in 1991. It is based on a legend depicted in Wimborne Minster about St Dunstan, one of the 'four saints of Wessex' and the patron saint of goldsmiths, whose emblem is a harp. It is said that the devil tried to tempt St Dunstan as he worked at his goldsmithing and, not wishing to be lured in this fashion, St Dunstan struck the devil with his red-hot tongs. The sculpture has been designed to depict St Dunstan as part of the harp on which the dragon sits.

As the month of October begins to fade away, Neil and his team at Knoll begin new projects, such as improving existing borders or clearing and planting the main rhododendron beds. Knoll is always evolving, and with its philosophy of creating maximum effect with minimum maintenance, together with keeping an eye on environmental and wildlife issues, there is much for the team to focus on.

All gardens are a balance with nature, but at Knoll it seems the custodians have come to an arrangement where they both respect each other. The result is a unique garden, full of surprise, interest and colour, which reflects the inspiration, dedication and enthusiasm of the award-winning team who care for it.

✳ Location: 2 miles/3.2 kilometres west of Ferndown off the A31 at Stapehill.
Further information: www.knollgardens.co.uk

357 RINGWOOD ROAD (LA CASITA DEL FLORES), FERNDOWN

It may well be, as the name 'La Casita del Flores' suggests, a little house, but the garden is certainly big on flowers, enthusiasm and talent. Home to Lyn and Malcolm Ovens, it immediately transports visitors from one of the south's busiest trunk roads – the garden is about 4 miles/ 6.4 kilometres north of the seaside town of Bournemouth – to the warm and colourful atmosphere of the Mediterranean. It was one of six finalists in the 2005 *Daily Mail* National Garden Competition.

When you enter the front garden (52 × 33 feet/16 × 10 metres), a cottage-style garden provides an array of colour. This is Lyn's preserve. Linger awhile and enjoy the fragrance and contrasting tones of the many perennial flowers. Her collection of clematis, lilies and fuchsias all compete for space as they provide a magnificent display in the central island bed and borders.

As you pass through the passageway leading to a Moorish keyhole door, the true extent of this couple's talents is unveiled. The walls are festooned with mosaics, painstakingly made by Lyn, depicting scenes from their Andalucian holidays. Malcolm takes the opportunity to display his photographs of wildlife and birds and close-ups of his many flowers.

The rear garden (40 × 33 feet/12 × 10.5 metres) is Malcolm's territory. This has a tropical theme, the planting reflecting memories of holidays overseas. A Chusan palm (*Trachycarpus fortunei*) sets the stage, supported by borders containing bananas, cannas, brugmansia, oleander, tree ferns, agaves, castor oil plant (*Ricinus communis*), dahlias and a host of other tender plants.

The rear garden with hexagonal raised bed with a tropical planting theme.

The lion's-head water feature behind the palm *Trachycarpus fortunei* and spiky-leaved *Agave americana* 'Variegata'.

Being situated close to Ferndown Common, a heathland habitat, the garden's soil is mainly sandy and in winter frost is a problem, as the soil does not retain heat. For this reason many of the exotic plants have been planted in pots, so that they can be removed to a safe haven – the conservatory – for the cold months.

The atmosphere in the garden is enhanced by the gentle sound of water as it trickles from the mouth of a lion's-head water feature, brought back from the pottery town of La Bisbal in northern Spain; and by a pebble pool with a recovered millstone purchased from nearby Bournemouth International Airport, where it was a feature inside and no longer required.

An aviary at the rear of the garden is the source of yet more sound and encourages wild birds to the garden, which Lyn feeds.

✱ Location: alongside the A348 Ringwood Road at Ferndown and about 4 miles/6.4 kilometres north of Bournemouth.

Further information: www.lynandmalc.co.uk

Summer colour in the cottage-style garden at the front of the house, with a tiled picture on the wall behind.

THE GLADE, FERNDOWN

Close to the busy urbanized infrastructure surrounding the area to the north of Bournemouth, The Glade is a sylvan retreat for its owners, Mary and Roger Angus. The landscaped garden in a tranquil setting offers woodland walks, a stream and a large wildlife pond, set amidst a variety of mature shrubs, trees, herbaceous plants and borders.

Working to a design concept they established some fifteen years ago with garden designer Kate Murdoch, Mary and Roger transformed the original 1¾-acre/0.7-hectare layout to complement the surrounding woodland and naturally sloping terrain. The landscaping created a horseshoe-shaped amphitheatre with large formal lawns. Spoil removed during the reconstruction was carefully relocated to form tiered terracing and banks.

Mary closely monitored the removal and relocation of existing plants from the excavated area, and ensured there was minimum encroachment or disturbance of the wildflower walks and shrubbery around the periphery. As a result, many mature specimens of camellia and rhododendron, and of less common species such as *Cornus florida*, stewartia and a magnificent example of kalmia, have been preserved. These have been complemented with newer planting.

In springtime, the wildflower walks are awash with wood anemones, primroses and bluebells, overhung with apple and cherry blossom, and the air is perfumed by yellow azaleas.

In 2001 Roger, who avoids digging, engaged contractors to convert the final untamed area of ditches and fallen timber at the northern end of the garden into a modest lake fed by a small stream with a series of cascades. Using a local dowser,

In summer roses adorn the house. The tree by the window is an albizia.

ABOVE A pink rhododendron reflected in The Glade's wildlife pond.
RIGHT The magnificent *Kalmia latifolia* flower and buds.

they successfully located an underground watercourse to ensure a natural source for these water features. A keen plantswoman, Mary took full advantage of the new planting opportunities, adding a bog garden containing gunneras, ferns, primulas, filipendula and purple loosestrife.

The garden and lake are surrounded by oak, ash, beech and birch trees, with willow, contorted hazel, albizia and *Dicksonia antarctica* for variety, all providing a home for birds, insects and other wildlife. Frogs, toads, grass snakes and even slow worms are often seen. Regular visitors include badgers, foxes and the occasional trespassing deer.

The garden is an oasis of calm and tranquillity, hidden away in the bustling heart of east Dorset. Mary and Roger want to keep the garden this way for as long as they can.

✱ Location: ¾ mile/ 1.2 kilometres north-east of Ferndown town centre near Trickett's Cross, approximately 8 miles/ 12.8 kilometres north of Bournemouth.

The woodland walk in spring.

COTTESMORE FARM, WEST MOORS

In a residential area only a short distance from the suburbs of Bournemouth, the garden at Cottesmore Farm offers the flavours of Australia and South America with a luxuriant tropical planting featuring many rare plants, all packed into only 1 acre/0.4 hectares. It is the creation of Paul and Valerie Guppy, formerly owners of High Hollow at nearby Corfe Mullen, which featured in the late Geoff Hamilton's television programme *Paradise Gardens*. They have made the garden around their new home in just twelve years.

A colourful display greets you as you enter the traditional cottage-garden-style front garden, backed by conifers, mixed shrubs and fruit trees and all brought together with a curving mown path. Just a short distance from the main property is a wildlife garden where the more exotic exhibits are displayed. A series of meticulously mown paths flow around large borders of herbaceous plants and annuals mixed with small conifers, shrubs and island beds of tropical plants.

Paul has used his experience as a propagator at Compton Acres to introduce, where possible, many varieties of palms, bananas, bamboos and tender plants, such as the Chilean bromeliad *Fascicularia*, and insert them among traditional grasses, red hot pokers (*Kniphofia*) and a host of perennials. In all there are over 100 palm trees of four species in the garden.

A visit to Cottesmore Farm also includes glimpses of rare-breed fowls – araucana and bearded d'Anvers – whose curiosity, when it overcomes them, causes them to make impromptu appearances between the plants in Valerie's wildlife garden – and indeed elsewhere!

A sweeping path takes you through the late summer colour of Cottesmore's traditional garden. Planting here includes *Thuja occidentalis* 'Emerald', *T.o.* 'Rheingold', *Gaillardia* × *grandiflora* 'Burgunder', penstemon, *Phlox paniculata*, *Lychnis coronaria* 'Alba', *Echinacea purpurea*, *Verbena hastata* and *Coreopsis* 'Sterntaler'.

LEFT ABOVE The herbaceous borders include *Cercis canadensis* 'Forest Pansy', *Gunnera manicata*, *Trachycarpus fortunei*, *Chusquea gigantea*, *Miscanthus sacchariflorus*, *Miscanthus sinensis* 'Variegatus' and *Eucomis* mixed species.

LEFT One of Cottesmore's colourful entrance borders, where the bright golden colours of *Choisya ternata* 'Sundance' (on the left) and *Thuja occidentalis* 'Rheingold' contrast with late summer flowers below.

A close-up of the border showing *Phyllostachys aurea*, *Helianthus* 'Lemon Queen', *Phlox paniculata, Persicaria amplexicaulis* and *Echium vulgare*.

✱ Location: 1 mile/ 1.6 kilometres north of West Moors off the B3072 Bournemouth to Verwood road.

EDMONDSHAM HOUSE, CRANBOURNE

Edmondsham, on the southern edge of Cranborne Chase, is one of the north Dorset villages once famous for their pottery because of the quality of the clay found in the region. Edmondsham House, described by Dorset writer Monica Hutchings as 'a beautiful house with gently rounded gables instead of the usual angular type and surrounded by parkland', is built on the site of a former manor mentioned in the Domesday Book, one of four manors here at the time.

The property has changed hands several times. The current house was built by Thomas Hussey, who acquired the property in 1563; there is also a Victorian dairy and stable block. The house has been home to Julia Smith since 1982, but it was in fact Julia's mother, Mary Medlycott, who was responsible for developing the 6-acre/2.4-hectare garden: she planted many of the spring bulbs that are one of its principal features today, and the shrubs and trees that complete the picture.

As you enter the gates, you drive past The Dell, which

LEFT A view of the house across the lawns with the wall surrounding the walled garden. The tree on the left is a black walnut (*Juglans nigra*).
BELOW Tulips 'Guiseppe Verdi' provide colour in the borders fronting the house during April.

has a small pond that often dries up in the summer, and a central island with a broad-leaved bamboo (*Sasa palmata*). In the foreground stands a dawn redwood (*Metasequoia glyptostroboides*) in all its glory, with a colourful reddish bark. The tree was once thought to be extinct and known only in fossil form; the 'dawn' in the common name refers to the 'dawn of time', and it was rediscovered in central China in 1941.

Overlooking the entrance are lime trees with large clumps of mistletoe clinging to their branches – mistletoe seems to be prolific in the area between Edmondsham and Cranborne. The limes contrast with a majestic cedar planted in the west lawn in 1848.

A circular banked area of lawn on the western side of the house is an unusual feature, said to have been used as an arena for cockfights in the Middle Ages. The main lawn in front of the house is more formal; in spring the eastern border exhibits tulips, in time for the Easter opening of the garden. Near the entrance to the Church of St Nicholas, which adjoins the grounds, a *Magnolia kobus* makes a spectacular springtime display.

Daffodils surround the foot of a copper beech tree. Beyond is the rich pastoral landscape of the estate.

A walled garden with herbaceous borders on either side is planted to provide a long season of interest, including peonies, oriental poppies, delphiniums, *Echinops*, *Eremurus*, verbena and asters. A long, narrow border to the right of the entrance gate includes *Scilla peruviana*, which flowers in early summer.

Following the appointment of head gardener Andrew Haynes in 1984, the walled kitchen garden is now cultivated organically, without the use of artificial chemical fertilizers or pesticides, with the enthusiastic support of Julia Smith, who is herself keen on nature conservation. Flowering plants mingle with the fruit and vegetables, so as to confuse pest insect species and to attract pollinating and beneficial insects.

In early spring drifts of daffodils appear around the garden, mingling with blue carpets of *Chionodoxa luciliae* while bluebells wait in the wings. In the ancient woodland surrounding the estate there is also a glorious display of wild naturalized daffodils, while below in the valley the River Crane, now reduced from its former glory to a small river, continues its journey through the rich landscape of north Dorset.

Edmondsham is one of the first gardens to open for viewing in the spring and visiting it is a most relaxing and pleasing experience. This may be because of its links with the past, which contribute to the homely and comfortable atmosphere; but it may also have something to do with its owner, who invites all visitors to enjoy the garden as if it were their own.

✻ Location: 9 miles/14.4 kilometres north-east of Wimborne Minster off the B3078.

4 NOEL ROAD, WALLISDOWN, BOURNEMOUTH

In a traditional English garden, sculptures and hard landscaping play a secondary or supporting role to the plants. Not so in Lesley and Ivor Pond's garden in Wallisdown near Bournemouth. In the last fifteen years (they have lived here for twenty-seven years), in between working in their business as hairdressers and wig makers, they have created a garden that represents their travels to the far eastern parts of China, and to Cambodia, Vietnam, Greece and crucially Rome through sculpture and architecture.

You may be surprised by the life-size statue of a Roman centurion in full regalia and armed with a *gladius* (sword) that greets you at the entrance, and the terracotta warrior standing sentry within. But you soon get into the swing of things when Ivor takes you up the hill past the nymphaeum – his grotto with cascading water, semi-clad statues and water nymphs – to his 'Roman' temple. Here, painted views of the Bay of Naples, Vesuvius and the Parthenon remind him of areas he particularly enjoyed while on holiday. Much of the temple he has constructed himself; it includes a full-size church window, which he purchased locally. Many of the statues he has had to import, no doubt at great expense, but nevertheless to great effect.

The journey back from the temple takes you past statues posing as water features and a Buddha in the lotus position with burning incense.

This is not, though, a garden without plants: it is filled with the bright colours of petunias, pelargoniums, lobelia, impatiens, fuchsias, begonias in June, July and August and

A general view of the garden with the nymphaeum or water garden at the centre and the temple behind.

NYMPHEUM

Soray, a marble stone statue imported from Ankor Wat, Cambodia, set amidst colourful impatiens, fuchsias, petunias and pelargoniums.

An atmospheric combination of statues and flowers, in constantly changing light. Morning glory climbs a statue and Surfinia petunias and begonias complete the picture.

includes hydrangeas and acers. A Roman garden is not complete without palm trees and you can see these as well. All this is packed into an area only 100 × 30 feet/30 × 9 metres.

✻ Location: 4 miles/6.4 kilometres north-east of Poole off the A3049.

Plants and statues surround the Roman temple.

46 ROSLIN ROAD SOUTH, BOURNEMOUTH

A garden designed with 'free spirit' is how Penny Slade, a former nurse and secretary to the East Dorset branch of Plant Heritage (formerly the National Council for the Conservation of Plants and Gardens), describes her ⅓ acre/0.13 hectares of walled garden, located in a quiet residential area just a short distance away from the centre of Bournemouth and the hustle and bustle of this seaside holiday resort and international conference and exhibition centre. Hers is a true plantswoman's garden, in which hard landscaping is replaced with ornamental grasses and angels' fishing rods (*Dierama pulcherrimum*), which provide structure and movement, and where plants take priority – the 'more the merrier', she says.

It has taken Penny twenty years to create this wonderful garden. During this time she has transformed a typical town plot with lawns and borders into a plant-lovers' paradise, so full of rare and unusual plants that now not a blade of grass can be seen. She has put her professional training to good use,

OPPOSITE A quiet resting place in the front gravel garden, where the sound of rustling giant feather grass (*Stipa gigantea*), seen here on the right, lends atmosphere and *Berkheya purpurea*, far left, provides splashes of colour amidst the many other plants.
BELOW *Pelargonium* 'Lord Bute'.

Allium sphaerocephalon.

Arum lily (*Zantedeschia aethiopica*) and *Dierama pulcherrimum.*

not in patient care but in the nurture – with considerable time and energy – of all the rare plants that grow in her three greenhouses and cold frames.

In the sunken south-facing front garden gravel pathways meander between waving dierama and ornamental grasses. It is a well-drained situation for sun-loving bulbs such as eucomis, dietes and agapanthus.

In the north-facing rear garden strategically placed flowerpots and an enclosed patio display an alternating show of unusual plants, while a raised octagonal bed containing grasses and dwarf conifers is backed by *Cornus capitata*

and *Alangium platanifolium*, in full bloom during July. One of the greenhouses is home to a spectacular collection of pelargoniums, while a border of dahlias, including *D.* 'My Love' and *D.* 'Smokey', has been neatly arranged outside. A small pond, safely protected from Penny's inquisitive grandchildren, and a fern corner add another dimension to this spectacular garden.

✳ Location: 1 mile/1.6 kilometres north-west of Bournemouth town centre off Glenferness Avenue.

The ornamental pond, designed with safety in mind.

CHINE VIEW, CASSEL AVENUE, WESTBOURNE

Chine View is the home of John and Jeannie Blay, who have lived here since 2001, and have progressively developed their ½-acre/0.2-hectare garden on a steeply banked, wooded coastal site near Bournemouth into a peaceful haven.

When they started the reconstruction of the garden, which is to the rear of the house, it consisted of an overgrown deep and narrow ravine or chine, which runs ultimately down to Poole Bay. Chines are a unique feature west of Bournemouth; others can be seen on the Isle of Wight. The Blays removed unwanted foliage and trees and disposed of the invasive *Rhododendron ponticum*, that pariah of the British countryside. When the digging and planting work began, the sides of the chine exposed a series of stepped and angled Purbeck stones, some of them weighing up to 3 tons (John estimates the total at around 330 tons), and the Blays incorporated these into the garden's construction.

Now as you enter the garden a serpentine-shaped lawn greets you; it is edged by a clipped hedge, with a Palladian-style rotunda at one end. As you walk round, you can't help noticing that John and Jeannie's talents extend beyond gardening to the many sculptures they have crafted themselves from wood, chicken wire and even cement, all strategically placed around the garden.

From the bottom of the garden looking back towards the house, you can see clearly many types of plants growing on the sides of the chine and around the edges: there are mature shrubs, including azaleas, rhododendrons, pieris and hydrangeas, which enjoy the acid to neutral soil (over a

From the house the deep chine beyond the formal lawn can be seen.

A Palladian-style rotunda, surrounded by palms, shaped box red-leaved pieris and colourful azaleas.

RIGHT ABOVE Dappled light plays on plants set among Purbeck stones.
RIGHT BELOW The bridge crossing the chine.

sub-base of sand and gravel), and numerous perennials. The Blays' intention is to expand the collection of subtropical plants. At the end of the garden, a bridge allows you to cross the chine and look down to the bottom.

✽ Location: 2 miles/3.2 kilometres west of Bournemouth off Alumhurst Road, Cassel Avenue, Westbourne.

24A WESTERN AVENUE, BRANKSOME PARK

A short distance inland from the golden beaches of Branksome Chine, between Poole and Bournemouth, is Branksome Park. One of the most prestigious and sought-after places in the south of England, the park was much loved by Sir John Betjeman, who urged readers of his classic book *Trains and Buttered Toast* to 'go to Bournemouth and more particularly to the exclusive Branksome. Here the pine trees and rhododendrons and heather are allowed to grow beside twisting roads . . . and houses live respectably among the foliage of their spacious gardens.'

Since 1976, 24a Western Avenue in Branksome Park has been home to Peter and Pauline Jackson. Given that they have a family interest in Burgon & Ball, a company with a pedigree of some 278 years that is dedicated to the manufacture of quality hand tools for the gardener, it is not surprising that they are interested in horticulture. They have worked tirelessly to create, from an area that was once heathland covered with *Rhododendron ponticum* and surrounded by maritime and Scots pine, a 1-acre/0.4-hectare garden that, with its use of lush foliage and exuberant hues, owes much to the influence of the late garden writer Christopher Lloyd.

Working with less than desirable soil – thin, free-draining and acidic, it is dry in summer and in areas waterlogged in winter – they have supplemented it with thirty years' worth of leaf mould and, in the rose garden, imported Somerset loam. This and a favourable microclimate have enabled them to construct a 'garden for all seasons', with many themes and variations, from traditional English to Mediterranean and

The colourful entrance to the cherry tree avenue. The planting includes blue agapanthus, pink *Pelargonium* 'Balcon' and in the foreground pale-leaved *Helichrysum petiolare*. On the right is a *Ficus* 'Brown Turkey'.

The borders and island beds are packed with unusual plants. The pines on the right are a traditional feature of the area.

subtropical, and where many species considered greenhouse plants flourish outdoors.

A gentle sloping driveway takes you to the front of the house and to a walled garden, past some of Peter's treasured and rare climbers, including the giant Burmese honeysuckle (*Lonicera hildebrandiana*) and *Mandevilla laxa*, strategically placed at the front door to provide a welcoming fragrance,

along with *Pandorea jasminoides*. This, together with many of the plants in the garden, has been sourced from some of the south's eminent nurserymen, including Norman Stanbrooke and John May, creator of Knoll Gardens (see page 144).

A step under the archway to the side of the house takes you through to the 'hot area' and a paved, Italian-style garden, which includes the warm colours of dahlias, cannas, the more exotic and unusual lion's ear plant (*Leonotis leonora*) from South Africa and *Tibouchina*, with its velvet leaves and luminous purple flowers. These grow beneath palms, cordylines and the bananas *Musa basjoo* and *Ensete*. The theme of lush foliage

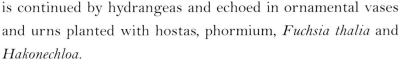
Glory lily (*Gloriosa superba* 'Rothschildiana').

is continued by hydrangeas and echoed in ornamental vases and urns planted with hostas, phormium, *Fuchsia thalia* and *Hakonechloa*.

On the south-facing side of the house, oleanders and *Trachelospermum jasminoides* flourish in front of a formal well-maintained lawn. This is surrounded by herbaceous borders awash with seasonal perennials and ornamental shrubs, and leads to the rose garden, where there are over 100 specimens of hybrid tea, floribunda and shrub roses. Here and in the woodland garden, Peter displays driftwood sculptures set off with ornamental grasses and pebbles.

A short walk into the woodland garden takes you past tree ferns (*Dicksonia antarctica* and *D. squarrosa*), a collection of bamboo, including the spectacular yellow canes of *Phyllostachys vivax aureocaulis*, 20 feet/6 metres high, and specimens of myrtle, one believed to have emanated from Queen Victoria's wedding bouquet. The tree collection includes a tulip tree (*Liriodendron tulipifera*), catalpa, azara, cercis, eucalyptus, gleditsia, magnolia and several acers, which shelter a wide

The giant Burmese honeysuckle (*Lonicera hildebrandiana*) provides a pleasant fragrance around any front door and here contrasts well with *Dahlia* 'Fascination' and its copper-coloured foliage.

variety of camellias, pieris, pittosporum and rhododendrons. Dry banks on the southern boundary host callistemon, echium, cistus, cytisus, *Genista aetnensis* and melaleuca, with agave, yucca, aloe, puya and fascicularia growing in the driest spots.

A walk along a cherry tree avenue – alas, the cherry trees have been reduced to just four over the years, but this loss has allowed *Crinodendron hookerianum*, *Acer palmatum* 'Senkaki', aralias and camellias to flourish – returns you to the front of the house, giving you a last chance to view the spectacular borders and island beds, packed with unusual plants and set

against a backdrop of palm trees – *Trachycarpus fortunei* and *Phoenix canariensis* – and eucalyptus. Prominent in the wall border are *Eriobotrya*, loquat and *Acacia baileyana* 'Purpurea'; and if you look closely you will see a *Sollya heterophylla* happily climbing with its delicate blue flowers through a 'Handel' rose.

Peter and Pauline set out to use their favourable microclimate to create a garden with the atmosphere of warmer latitudes, using plants with strong structure, foliage and a wide colour palette. Without doubt they have achieved this, with resounding success.

✱ Location: 3 miles/4.8 kilometres west of Bournemouth off Canford Cliffs Road.

Left to right: *Drepanostachyum falconeri*, *Canna iridifolia*, *Crocosmia*, *Ensete ventricosum* 'Maurelii', *Cosmos* 'Sonata Pink', *Dahlia* 'Hillcrest Royal' and at the back, with the woodland garden behind, *Fatsia japonica*.

Echinacea purpurea 'Rubinstern' with the grass *Miscanthus* 'Ferner Osten' in the summer border.

COMPTON ACRES, CANFORD CLIFFS

The garden at Compton Acres was made in 1920 by the businessman Thomas William Simpson, a margarine entrepreneur whose interest in horticulture and overseas travel inspired him to create a 'garden with a difference' – essentially a series of themed gardens – at his seaside home. Simpson appointed the well-respected Mr Albert Middleton as head gardener, to oversee the garden's construction, and the 10-acre/4-hectare heathland site – on a beautiful hilltop close to the village of Canford Cliffs between Poole, Bournemouth and the beaches of Sandbanks – was transformed: the wilderness of gorse and heather and slopes densely clad with Scots pines turned into a unique representation of the world's gardens. The cost of the construction was in the region of £220,000, roughly the equivalent of £10 million today – a huge amount considering that it was a private garden.

Today Compton Acres is possibly the most publicized and photographed garden in Dorset. Following the war years, however, when gardeners were called to 'dig for Britain' and labour was in short supply, the gardens began to fall into disrepair – until 1950, when the architect J.S. Beard purchased the property. He introduced his own planting style, and also created a circular Purbeck stone picnic garden as a memorial to his son Dick, who was killed while flying with the Royal Air Force, and two of his young daughters, who died from polio. In 1964 Mr John Brady and his wife bought the gardens and began opening them to the public, eventually selling them in 1985.

Compton Acres is currently owned by Bernard and Kaye

The Italian Garden, reflected in the Fountain Pool. *Nymphaea* 'Gloriosa' floats on the surface while *Begonia* 'Lotto Scarlet' provides striking colour.

At the end of the fountain pool in the Italian Garden is an ornamental tempietto. *Begonia* 'Lotto Scarlet' lines the pool and in the pots are *Begonia* 'Fiery Red' with *Scaerola* 'Sapphire'.

Merna. To the gratitude of all who visit it, these owners respect this historic garden not only for its horticultural interest but also as an important visitor attraction in the area. The care and restoration of the garden is under the control of the Compton Acres gardening team, advised by Peter Thoday, a former horticultural director at the Eden Project in Cornwall, and Mary Payne MBE, gardening broadcaster, lecturer and designer.

The Italian Garden, the first of the main themed gardens, displays the essential elements of Italian landscape design with symmetry and formality. It includes statuary, an ornamental pond with a central fountain, and a spectacular display of seasonal bedding plants. The colour and reflections in this part of the garden continue to be a main feature of Compton Acres.

It is a short walk through to the Palm Court, which has a Mediterranean appearance with central palms (*Trachycarpus fortunei*) surrounded by densely planted seasonal borders.

A meandering pathway takes you through the Wooded Valley, where there are traditional woodland plants such as bluebells

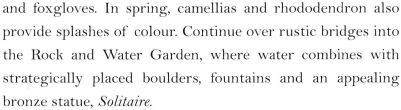

and foxgloves. In spring, camellias and rhododendron also provide splashes of colour. Continue over rustic bridges into the Rock and Water Garden, where water combines with strategically placed boulders, fountains and an appealing bronze statue, *Solitaire*.

On reaching the refreshment area and nearby viewpoint, stop and admire the grand views over Poole Harbour, the second largest natural harbour in the world, and beyond to the Purbeck hills. You can also see Brownsea Island, famed for its links with the Scout movement, where in 1907 Baden-Powell set up his experimental camp, which was to be the beginning of worldwide scouting.

Paths wind through the gardens amidst shrubs, trees and foliage, with the ever-present pines, so characteristic of the area, providing dappled light and shade.

The Heather Garden, with its collection of native moorland heathers, is surrounded by rhododendron hedges and interspersed with conifers and deciduous trees. Two statues, *The Poet* and *The Peasant*, take pride of place within the display.

The Japanese Garden takes you to the Far East with many of the features that can be seen in a traditional Japanese

ABOVE A light sprinkling of snow adds atmosphere to the Japanese Garden, which was constructed by Thomas Simpson following a visit to the gardens in Kyoto; buildings, artefacts, plants and even fish were exported from Japan under licence.

RIGHT ABOVE *The Poet* and *The Peasant* in the Heather Garden.
RIGHT BELOW Early spring in the Rock and Water Garden.

garden. An elegant imperial teahouse sits beside a large lake surrounded by acers, azaleas and rhododendrons. A *Wisteria sinensis* overhangs the teahouse, casting dynamic reflections in the water below. A pagoda sits at one end of the lake and carefully placed stepping stones allow safe passage across to it (an alternative route is available for the faint-hearted). No Japanese garden would be complete without a Buddha and lanterns, which originate from an earlier Chinese culture: these and many authentic artefacts can be found here.

Today at Compton Acres there is a continuing programme of redevelopment, horticultural conservation and restoration.

The Wooded Valley has undergone extensive tree work and the Rock and Water Garden has seen the replanting of more than 200 different taxa. New areas are always being created: the most recent are an area of Australasian plants and a subtropical garden with walks through bamboo and Moutan peonies. It remains a superlative series of gardens in one location that collectively achieve its creator's dream of a 'garden with a difference'.

✳ Location: 2 miles/3.2 kilometres east of Poole on Canford Cliffs Road.

Further information: www.comptonacres.co.uk

Stepping stones and reflections in the Japanese Garden.

INDEX

Dahlia 'Fashion Monger'.

ACKNOWLEDGEMENTS

I trust readers of this book will appreciate the time and energy expended by all those who have so kindly allowed me access to their innermost sanctuaries. Without their generous help this book would not have been possible.

I would particularly like to thank my wife Beryl for her loyal support throughout the project, and Phil Wills and his wife Jean for their tremendous help and assistance. From its early conception to final preparation Phil was both a knowledgeable asset and carrier of photographic equipment, a task performed with his customary enthusiasm and sense of humour.

Along the streamside walk through the woodland glades at Minterne.